WHAT
GOD HAS
PROMISED
YOU

STEPHEN A. MCALLISTER

WHAT GOD HAS PROMISED YOU

ANCIENT WISDOM FOR MODERN TIMES

REFLECTIONS FOR INDIVIDUAL
AND GROUP STUDY
FROM PAUL'S EPISTLE TO THE ROMANS

Published by
BPS books
Toronto, Canada, and New York
bpsbooks.com
A division of Bastian Publishing Services Ltd.

ISBN 978-1-926645-08-7

Library of Congress
Control Number: 2009909960

Canadian Cataloguing-in-Publication data available from Library and Archives Canda.

Cover design: Gnibel
Text design and typesetting: Kinetics Design, kdbooks.ca

To the men and women

whose life stories are featured in this book.

Each person has lived a life that truly shows

what God has promised.

CONTENTS

God's
Gospel — Good news
Gospel — Good news
Unveils — Revealed.
God's
Righteousness —

PREFACE

THIS book was conceived over six years ago when I was serving as the minister of a suburban church in Toronto, Ontario. I was preparing a series of homilies for the summer services and felt called to preach on the Epistle to the Romans. When I told some of my friends what I was doing they said, "Why do you want to work so hard? No one does that in the summer time!"

Not long after that I took a break from parish ministry and enrolled full time in the Ecumenical Doctor of Ministry program at Catholic Theological Union in Chicago. During this time, the early material that would become the basis of this book "sat" as I immersed myself in the seminary's rich environment of culture and wisdom, studying with men and women from around the world. (Some of their stories, albeit with identities changed, have made their way into the final form of this book.)

After I returned to Toronto I was asked by a United Church to lead two Bible-study groups using my reflections on Romans. Since then a Pentecostal church has completed an expanded study using the material, and a group of laypeople in a United Church in Prince Edward Island is in its second year of using the study. With the encouragement of many people who attended these studies, I added new material and began working to complete the book.

Two recent events encouraged me as I finished the book. In the spring of 2009, I attended a church in the Fellowship of Christian Assemblies, USA, in Chicago. To my surprise, the minister was beginning a sermon series on Romans. I was heartened to learn of the interest of his congregation. The congregation had made a commitment to follow the weekly teaching sermons and then share their personal study experiences in weekly small group meetings. Shortly after that, a friend told me that he was volunteering his time each week as a Bible-study leader with a group of seniors at a retirement home. His study was entitled "Roaming Around Romans." He reported that the group was faithful in attendance and was finding Romans to be particularly enlightening and enjoyable. I trust that the same will prove true for you.

Allow me to leave this thought with you as you begin to read this book. The Bible says that Samuel, prior to anointing Saul ruler over the people of Israel, said to him, "… stop here … for a while, that I may make known to you the word of God" (1 Sam. 9:27). I make the same invitation to you: Stop here for a while and discover for yourself what God has promised you. Seek God's will for your life, because God's promises are true, forever and ever!

Blessings,
Stephen

How to Use This Book

I AM delighted that you wish to know more about Paul's Epistle to the Romans. You may be new to Christanity. You may be a faithful church attendee, or you may have left the church long ago. No matter what your current faith stance, or your religious affiliation, you will find treasure in this book that may affect your life in a very positive way.

Paul's epistle has changed the lives of many people and has provided a strong theological and practical foundation for the Christian Church. Although I cover only eight of its sixteen chapters, I encourage you to read the entire epistle when you have the time. You will be richly blessed.

What God Has Promised You is not intended to test your Bible knowledge but to give you an opportunity to delve more deeply into these particular words of the Bible: to learn, ask questions, and grow in faith. Engage in this study for the pure pleasure of concentrating on short passages of scripture and sharing your faith journey with family and friends.

This book may be used for individual study, group study, or both.

If you plan to read it on your own, you can build this into your normal devotion time. However, if a daily commitment is too difficult for you to schedule, set aside a short block of time in your week to read the material.

Either way, find a place where you can read and think without distraction.

Perhaps light a candle, pour yourself a cup of tea, and begin. Think about the questions at the beginning and end of each chapter and how they apply to your life. You may want to keep a journal as you work through this study. Reading, writing, prayer, and meditation in combination make for a powerful way to grow in faith.

Desiree LaBine

If you are a member of a group setting out to study this book, read the chapters individually as described above and then come together regularly for review and discussion. Each chapter describes a key promise that God has made and includes a brief section for those who wish to delve more deeply into the theological issues that Paul addresses. These sections are meant to open up the issue for deeper investigation.

Between the questions for reflection at the beginning and end of each chapter is a meditation based on the Romans passage, which may help you to engage the material personally or in group reflection and discussion. Each chapter also includes a story of a person or couple whose faith journey truly exemplifies God's promise for

their life in connection with the particular reading from
Romans. In all cases, the stories are true but the identities
of the people have been changed.

INTRODUCTION

A S many times as I have read the Epistle to the
Romans, I am always amazed at the richness and
depth of Paul's wisdom. The Apostle Paul wrote this
letter sometime in the middle to the late 50s of the first
century, probably while planning a trip to Jerusalem
with the intention of going on to Rome and then to
Spain.[1] The epistle is special among his writings. N.T.
Wright, in his commentary on the epistle, says, "Romans
is neither a systematic theology nor a summary of Paul's
lifework, but it is by common consent his masterpiece.
It dwarfs most of his other writings, an Alpine peak
towering over hills and villages."[2]

The epistle contains many of the familiar phrases that
some Christians know by heart:

> **5:8:** But God proves his love for us in that while we
> still were sinners Christ died for us.

> **8:18:** I consider that the sufferings of this present
> time are not worth comparing with the glory about
> to be revealed to us.

> **8:28:** We know that all things work together for good
> for those who love God, who are called according to
> his purpose.

1 *The New Interpreter's Bible*, X, 396.
2 *Ibid.*, 395.

8:35: Who will separate us from the love of Christ? Will hardship, or distress, or persecution, or famine, or nakedness, or peril, or sword?

10:9-10: because if you confess with your lips that Jesus is Lord and believe in your heart that God raised him from the dead, you will be saved. For one believes with the heart and so is justified, and one confesses with the mouth and so is saved.

Romans addresses many of the issues with which modern-day Christians struggle: righteousness, sin, grace, faith, justice, love, hope, and salvation, to name but a few. Paul knew there were challenges within the church community in Rome. He sent this letter to share the necessity of giving one's life to God in faith, as had the great patriarch of faith, Abraham. Paul also shares his profound wisdom about how people in communities, particularly those who call themselves "people on the way," followers of Christ, should treat others.

The first chapter of this book begins with Paul's thoughts on the faithfulness of Abraham and how we are called to live our lives with Abraham-like faith and unwavering belief. I discuss the rat race of our lives and how it affects our ability to live as God would have us live. I explore Paul's idea of "righteousness" and how we are called into a restored relationship with God.

I shared part of chapter 2 as a sermon given at a downtown church in Newfoundland. I will never forget the woman who told me how this sermon changed her life. She said, "I needed to hear the words 'don't give up' because of my struggles earlier this year." Maybe you too have needed to hear God's promises during times of trial in your life. We often become burdened with the sins of our past and forget God's promise that we will be forgiven through faith in Christ. This chapter explores the concepts of forgiveness and justification.

Chapter 3 considers God's promise of new and abundant life in Christ and Christ's desire for us to walk in "newness of life." This chapter also presents the teaching of the prophet Jeremiah and his words about the sin of the people that is "written with an iron pen; with a diamond point it is engraved on the tablet of their hearts" (Jer. 17:1).

The Apostle Paul is well aware of humanity's propensity to sin. He addresses the issue forthrightly, asking and then answering the question in the same breath: "Who will rescue me ...? Thanks be to God through Jesus Christ our Lord!" (Rom. 7:24-25) Chapter 4 briefly examines the conversion stories of three men: John Wesley, the founder of Methodism; John Newton, a former slave runner; and the Apostle Paul. These stories show how God rescues those who are lost. Sin is the focus of the theological reflection.

Chapter 5 widens our study to take in Paul's thinking on the power of the Holy Spirit to restore our lives. The theological reflection in this chapter talks about the Holy Spirit. The message looks at the power of God's word to transform lives. It highlights the life and work of Johann Sebastian Bach, showing how the eighth chapter of Romans inspired one of his masterpieces, *Jesu, meine Freude*.

Chapter 6 explores the theological issue of suffering. It includes part of the life story of Dietrich Bonhoeffer, as well as a story told to Max Lucado by his Portuguese-language teacher during his time in Brazil. The Apostle Paul reminds us that no matter what we go through in life, "All will be revealed" (Rom. 8:18). The chapter ends with a true-life story of a nun from East Africa whose personal story shows how God's revealed glory far exceeds the present suffering. No one escapes suffering. The Lord himself told us that the road to salvation runs alongside the road of suffering. This is so because the true life of faith will take us into the world of the poor and the oppressed, because Jesus lived to bring hope to the poor and good news to the oppressed. Jesus himself suffered unto death so that all might know God's exorbitant love.

As much as God's promises are real, and lives throughout the generations bear witness to the power of God's love in this world, we are prone to living a life of spiritual complacency. This is not new. The prophet Zephaniah wrote about the complacency of his people more than twenty-five hundred years ago. "At that time I will search Jerusalem with lamps, and I will punish the people who rest complacently on their dregs ..." (Zeph. 1:12). Chapter 7, "Complacency or Commitment?", takes a brief look at the worldwide decline in interest in Christianity, particularly in North America. The chapter introduces some of Pierre Berton's findings in *The Comfortable Pew*, as current as the day he wrote the book some forty-five years ago. The issue of covenant is explored in the theology section.

Chapter 8 takes a trip to the icecap of Antarctica to explore the family dynamics of emperor penguins. This exciting chapter explores the theological concept of "call" – of how we are called to bring the good news of Christ to the world. As Paul says, "How beautiful are the feet of those who bring good news!" (Rom. 10:15)

Chapter 9 describes three key areas that churches should seek to improve. It explores Paul's desire for Christian communities to live together in worship, holiness, and unity. I first shared this message with a Presbyterian congregation that was exploring new ways to be faithful to God's call on their church. The chapter ends with the true story of a couple who continue to bless their church by helping people live out God's promise that their gifts are truly valued.

The final chapter of the book examines the most difficult challenge that faces us as men and women today: how to love those who hurt us, how to forgive the unforgivable, and how to repay evil with love (Rom. 12:21). The true story of a prison chaplain exemplifies the power of God's word and forgiveness to change lives and bring hope to those with no hope. The chapter ends with a paraphrase of the statement from the mid-1960s television series *Mission Impossible*: "As usual, should you or any member of your community feel discouraged, Jesus Christ our Lord will be with you until the end of the age. The Spirit of the Lord is upon you."

Desiree LaBine

1

Unwavering Belief

Romans 4:13-25

Romans 4:13-25

¹³For the promise that he would inherit the world did not come to Abraham or to his descendants through the law but through the righteousness of faith. ¹⁴If it is the adherents of the law who are to be the heirs, faith is null and the promise is void. ¹⁵For the law brings wrath; but where there is no law, neither is there violation. ¹⁶For this reason it depends on faith, in order that the promise may rest on grace and be guaranteed to all his descendants, not only to the adherents of the law but also to those who share the faith of Abraham (for he is the father of all of us, ¹⁷as it is written, "I have made you the father of many nations") – in the presence of the God in whom he believed, who gives life to the dead and calls into existence the things that do not exist. ¹⁸Hoping against hope, he believed that he would become "the father of many nations," according to what was said, "So numerous shall your descendants be." ¹⁹He did not weaken in faith when he considered his own body, which was already as good as dead (for he was about a hundred years old), or when he considered the barrenness of Sarah's womb. ²⁰No distrust made him waver concerning the promise of God, but he grew strong in his faith as he gave glory to God, ²¹being fully convinced that God was able to do what he had promised. ²²Therefore his faith "was reckoned to him as righteousness." ²³Now the words, "it was reckoned to him," were written not for his sake alone, ²⁴but for ours also. It will be reckoned to us who believe in him who raised Jesus our Lord from the dead, ²⁵who was handed over to death for our trespasses and was raised for our justification.

to bring us back to God.

2

GOD'S PROMISE

*Place your trust in God and God
will direct your path.*

ROMANS 4:20

FOCUS

The faithfulness of Abraham.

THEOLOGICAL BACKGROUND

In this passage Paul writes about righteousness (Rom.
4:13, 22) and justification (Rom. 4:25). Paul knows that the
righteousness of God is revealed through faith for faith. He
writes earlier in the epistle, "The one who is righteous will
live by faith."[3] He believed that the people of Israel had
strayed from their covenant relationship with God, who
had promised to be faithful.

Paul believes that the righteousness of God (δικαιοσυνη
θεου) is the expectation that God would be faithful to the
patriarchs. Righteousness was loyalty to the covenant. He
also believed that the justice of God (θεου δικαιοσυνην)
"set to rights that which is out of joint, restoring things
as they should be."[4] Interestingly, the words *justice*
and *righteousness* come from the same Greek word,
δικαιοσυνη. In the biblical context, justice does not mean
punishment but a restoration of right relationship with
God. Justice means doing what God requires: righting
wrongs and establishing right relationships.

3

---

3 *The New Oxford Annotated Bible*, Rom. 1:16-17. (Unless otherwise
  noted, all scripture references are from the New Revised Standard
  Version.)
4 *The New Interpreter's Bible*, X, 399.

Paul believes that the covenant relationship established between God and the people of Israel is also intended for the whole human race, which needs to be rescued from evil and corruption. Whereas God's covenant with Israel was meant "to address the problem of human sin and the failure of creation as a whole to be what its creator had intended it to be, the covenant was the means of bringing God's justice to the whole world."[5]

OPENING REFLECTIONS

How do you understand God's will for your life?

What are God's promises in your life? Do you believe these promises?

---

5 *Ibid.*

MEDITATION ON THE PROMISE

YOU may have seen the movie *Rat Race*, an updated version of *It's a Mad, Mad, Mad, Mad World* (1963). In *Rat Race* a billionaire Las Vegas casino owner (played by John Cleese) sets up a gambling scheme in which bettors wage on which of six candidates will find the $2 million that he has hidden somewhere in a locker. The cross-country race to find this treasure is driven by the contestants' desire to become instantly wealthy.

A rat race, according to the *Random House Unabridged Dictionary*, is "any exhausting, unremitting, and usually competitive activity or routine, especially a pressured urban working life spent trying to get ahead with little time left for leisure, contemplation, etc." Many people describe their lives as a rat race, especially those living in major cities. As a result of the recent meltdown of the U.S. sub-prime market and the global shock experienced by many of the world's leading banks, governments have pledged hundreds of billions of dollars to support the banks, leading to a future that is impossible to predict. In events that no one would have considered possible, Chrysler Corporation and General Motors faced bankruptcy proceedings in the United States and Canada. Hundreds of dealerships will be closed as the industry consolidates. That is not to mention the day-to-day financial pressures people are facing because of the closure of manufacturing plants and the increasing costs of fuel and food.

Today our rat race is fuelled by a full-time economic engine that demands high performance and squeezes as much out of workers as they can give. Many people work in the retail sector and have to juggle seven-day work shifts. Others work in jobs where they have to go to the office on Saturdays or Sundays to take care of a special project or to get caught up because the work *just can't wait*. Many people in affluent areas of the world own a laptop computer, a Blackberry, a cell phone, a pager, a PDA, or an iPhone. Their homes may be equipped with high-speed Internet and a wireless network. They are never disconnected from work. Teenagers are not immune to technological stress. According to the Nielsen Company, teenagers in the United States sent and received an average of 2,272 text messages per month in the fourth quarter of 2008. "Physicians and psychologists say it is leading to anxiety, distraction in school, failing grades, repetitive stress, injury, and sleep deprivation."[6] No wonder life feels stressful. Welcome to the rat race of modern-day society: financial pressure, demanding work schedules, and not enough time to live a balanced life.

Paul speaks about the faith of Abraham, who at the age of seventy-five left his familiar circumstances to follow God's call. I can hardly imagine leaving house and home,

---

6 Katie Hafner, "Texting May Be Taking a Toll," *New York Times*, May 25, 2009.

family and friends, stability and routine for a journey into the unknown at that age. One person told me, "I wouldn't do that at the age of sixty-five let alone seventy-five." Abraham and his family left the city of Ur, located in what is now southern Iraq, and travelled approximately one thousand kilometers with their herds and entourage. Imagine the logistical challenge of feeding and watering so many animals and people on such a long journey.

It is one thing to leave home to go to school or work, or to get married and move out, but when you're seventy-five? How many of your parents or grandparents would even *think* of such a journey?

A few years ago, I was leading a Bible study on the story of Abraham and Sarah as found in the book of Genesis (11:27-12:9). After we read about Abraham and Sarah's faith, a woman said to me, "God must have spoken more clearly to people in Bible days." Another person replied immediately, "Yes, God speaks, but we do not hear because we do not listen." "The Bible says that God spoke to Abraham at the 'crossroads' of his life."[7] "Now the Lord said to Abram, 'Go from your country and your kindred and your father's house to the land that I will show you' " (Gen. 12:1). Why did God choose an old man – why him at all? God's reason is not humanly discernible.[8]

God casts his favour on Abraham, even though the Bible says nothing of Abraham's righteousness. He is asked to do what we would say is impossible. The text begins with a command from God, "Go," and not to a place he knew but to "the land that I will show you." Abraham left his home and security to go into the unknown simply with his faith and the faith of his family. Abraham's "yes" was a human response to the divine will. He could have said "no

7 *The Torah*, 90.
8 *Ibid.*, 93.

way," as many do. Abraham was open to God's desire and God opened the future to him and his family, and to future generations.

> *"Trust in the LORD with all your heart, and lean not on your own understanding; in all your ways acknowledge Him, And He shall direct your paths."*
> –Prov. 3:5-6, KJV

You may feel that you are at the crossroads of life, not really knowing where the path of life will take you. You may have a short-term goal to work, study, or travel. You may have met the soul mate of your dreams and have thoughts of marriage, or you may look into the future and say, "I have no idea what I should do." You may be retired or facing retirement, wondering what you will do with your time. In all these matters you can choose to experience life as a rat race or to find better balance in your life: time for work, play, and rest, for family and friends, and for your spiritual needs.

In *Rat Race*, unbeknownst to the contestants, John Cleese has a group of rich people watching the race and betting money on who would win. In the end, no one wins. Nor will any of us win by chasing after false gods.

Abraham was not caught up in a rat race. While some may have felt that he was crazy, he chose to listen to God's call and travel into the unknown. He did not focus on the things we think important. Abraham had incredible faith!

Paul writes to the church in Rome about Abraham's faith. Abraham did not undertake the cross-country journey to get rich but simply to follow God's will for him and his family. Paul writes, "For the promise that he would be the heir of the world was not to Abraham or to his seed through the law, but through the righteousness of faith" (Rom. 4:13). "And not being weak in faith, he did not consider his own body, already dead (since he was about a hundred years old), and the deadness of Sarah's womb. He did not waver at the promise of God through unbelief, but was strengthened in faith, giving glory to God" (Rom. 4:19-20, NKJV).

This is the faith by which Christians are called to believe. We share in this faith not because of our ancestry, our birthplace, or our economic status in life, but because we are a part of a community of faith, bound together by one thing and one thing only. What is that one thing? As Paul writes, it is believing "on him that raised up Jesus our Lord from the dead. Who was delivered for our offenses, and was raised again for our justification" (Rom. 4:24-25, KJV). N.T. Wright's commentary says of this passage, "There is no room, as far as Paul is concerned, for that impossible hybrid, a Christian who does not believe in the resurrection of Jesus."[9]

We are called to share Abraham's faith in the same God who led him to be the father of many nations, the One who raised Jesus from the dead, and the One who will bring us into a renewed relationship with God. None of us really knows what lies ahead on this journey of life. We can choose to engage in the rat race, or we can refocus our life to discern and follow God's will. As was the case with Abraham and his family, trusting in God will involve a measure of risk and uncertainty.

With Abraham-like faith in a loving God made known through his son Jesus Christ, we will experience many blessings on *our* journeys into the unknown. This is what God has promised! Abraham moved forward into the future with unwavering belief, believing in God's promise. If *you* place your trust in God, God will direct *your* path.

---

9 *The New Interpreter's Bible*, X, 507.

CLOSING REFLECTIONS

Pastor Daniels grew up in the warmth of the Caribbean sun. Early in his life, many knew that he was destined to serve God. Like many who receive God's call, however, Pastor Daniels resisted the call for a long time. In God's time he responded to the call and subsequently immigrated to Canada where he met his wife and later planted a church.

Today Pastor Daniels and his wife shepherd a thriving church and support numerous overseas missions. Pastor Daniels is a spiritual father to many congregations, pastors, and indeed nations. He and his family have received God's promise of the inheritance "through faith alone." Like Abraham and Sarah, they have endured much, yet in God's time they have received the fruit of the promise. They placed their total trust in God and God has directed their path.

When you read Pastor Daniels' true-life story, what do you think it means to have the faith of Abraham?

Paul says that Abraham "hoping against hope believed."
How do you think Pastor Daniels and his wife understand
this depth of faith?

"My life is a rat race." Share your thoughts with others.

How has God has done the impossible in your life?

2

DON'T GIVE UP

Romans 5:1-8

Romans 5:1-8

¹Therefore, since we are justified by faith, we have peace with God through our Lord Jesus Christ, ²through whom we have obtained access to this grace in which we stand; and we boast in our hope of sharing the glory of God. ³And not only that, but we also boast in our sufferings, knowing that suffering produces endurance, ⁴and endurance produces character, and character produces hope, ⁵and hope does not disappoint us, because God's love has been poured into our hearts through the Holy Spirit that has been given to us. ⁶For while we were still weak, at the right time Christ died for the ungodly. ⁷Indeed, rarely will anyone die for a righteous person – though perhaps for a good person someone might actually dare to die. ⁸But God proves his love for us in that while we still were sinners Christ died for us.

GOD'S PROMISE

God will be with you in all circumstances.

ROMANS 5:8

FOCUS

Faithful living and suffering.

THEOLOGICAL BACKGROUND

Paul often uses the word *justification*. What does it mean to be justified? It means to be acquitted or forgiven. When God forgives, he erases the record of our past sins and we begin life with a clean slate. Being justified is a gift of God's grace. It cannot be earned by working harder.

How do we receive this acquittal? Simple – by turning our life over to Christ, in faith! Paul tells us clearly that "redemption is in Christ Jesus" (Rom. 3:24-26). He also tells us that God demonstrates his love for us in that "while we still were sinners Christ died for us" (Rom. 5:8). The following Bible verses describe God's forgiveness:

Psalm 130:3-4: If you, O LORD, should mark iniquities, Lord, who could stand? But there is forgiveness with you, so that you may be revered.

Acts 5:31: God exalted him at his right hand as Leader and Savior that he might give repentance to Israel and forgiveness of sins.

Colossians 1:13-14: He has rescued us from the power of darkness and transferred us into the kingdom of his beloved Son, in whom we have redemption, the forgiveness of sins.

OPENING REFLECTIONS

What does it mean to "give up" at home, work, school, or church?

Membership and attendance at worship in many Christian churches is declining. Why do you think this is so? What can be done about it?

MEDITATION ON THE PROMISE

PAUL writes about hope by addressing the issue of suffering. This makes sense because suffering can cause us to give up hope. Here is Paul's insight into suffering: "... suffering produces endurance, and endurance produces character, and character produces hope, and hope does not disappoint us, because God's love has been poured into our hearts through the Holy Spirit that has been given to us" (Rom. 5:3-5).

Paul was writing to the *church* in Rome, not directly to individuals. He assumed that the church was the place where people would hear this good news. Can the church be a place of hope for you today? For many it has lost its ability to be relevant and as such offers no hope. In the 1980s many church people began to sense that something was wrong. Their solution was to work harder at what they were already doing. By the 1990s even the secular press was highlighting major problems faced by mainline liberal denominations. People by the millions have given up on church. We have seen the decline all over North America, although some congregations are growing. In the 2001 Canadian Census, over 1.8 million people in Ontario reported "no religious affiliation."[10] Canadian educator and theologian Douglas John Hall, searching for an explanation, expresses Martin Luther's belief that the church has become corrupt by going after "power for itself by prostituting itself with the powerful and not remaining

17

---

10 McAllister, *Revival of Wexford Heights United Church*, 67.

faithful to the weak, crucified Christ!"[11] For many people, the church has forgotten how to offer grace instead of judgment. How approachable is your church when you have problems? Is the church the place where you share your burdens?

Philip Yancey begins his book *What's So Amazing About Grace?* with the story of a prostitute who visits a person who works with the down and out in Chicago.[12] After she tells this man her sad story he asks her, "Did you ever think of going to a church for help?" Yancey reports this worker as saying, "I will never forget the look of pure, naïve shock that crossed her face." The worker says the woman responded with, "Church ... Why would I ever go there? I was already feeling terrible about myself. They'd just make me feel worse."[13] What struck Yancey when he heard this story was that "women, much like this prostitute, fled toward Jesus, not away from him. The worse a person felt about herself, the more likely she saw Jesus as a refuge. Has the church lost that gift? Evidently the down-and-out, who flocked to Jesus when he lived on earth, no longer feel welcome among his followers."[14]

I believe that some people in the institutional church have forgotten the grace-filled ministry of Christ and thus have lost the ability to serve those who have lost hope. Paul reminds us that "God proves his love for us in that while we still were sinners Christ died for us" (Rom. 5:8). Many of your friends may have given up on church. You

---

11 Hall, *Why Christian?*,132. Hall, *Bound and Free*, 85:
  When Christianity allowed itself to become the darling of power structures, dominant races and classes, and established systems (and that is what Christendom is all about), it lost its capacity to be there for the whole, and especially those parts of the whole creaturely context that were victimized by the very power structures that the Christians were so keen to court.
12 Philip Yancey, *What's So Amazing About Grace?*
13 *Ibid.*, 11.
14 *Ibid.*

yourself may have considered leaving church or maybe you already have. You may wish to read another book by Yancey, *Church, Why Bother?*

It is easy to give up on church, similar to how we can become discouraged or sidetracked in life. We can get so busy that we lose all sense of balance, shuffling some areas of our lives, such as our personal faith life, to the bottom of our priority list. When life gets difficult, we may feel like giving up. Some of us may have experienced defeat in our lives and may have already given up. It is easy to give up!

Abraham Lincoln, a famous and respected political leader, faced many setbacks in his life, yet he did not give up. Lincoln was defeated in his first try for the state legislature; defeated in his desire to become commissioner of the General Land Office; defeated in a contest for a seat the United States Senate; defeated for the vice presidency of the United States; defeated in an effort to become a junior senator from Illinois. Despite five political losses, he was elected president of the United States in 1860.[15] The great Russian writer Leo Tolstoy flunked out of college, yet he did not give up.[16] When he learned that Lincoln had died, he remarked, "Lincoln was a Christ in miniature."[17] That is a powerful tribute to a man who knew much defeat, a man who must have lived an incredibly busy life – a man who did not give up!

Some people get so discouraged or depressed that they give up on life and commit suicide. In the past few years I have conducted the funerals of several men in their early fifties who died at their own hands. How can we make sense of these tragedies? Suicide affects young people as well. Several years ago a first-year student at Queen's University, Kingston, Ontario, called me to share her pain

15 Jones and Jones, *500 Illustrations*. 25.
16 *Ibid.*
17 *Ibid.*, 57.

and shock. A fellow student had committed suicide. Why did this happen? Perhaps there was too much pressure, a fear of failure, or a sense of shame. If you ever feel suicidal or know of "people on the edge," please reach out for help. Life is precious. Hindsight is likely to show that our failures are not as big as we imagine them at the time.

Despite all of the Apostle Paul's physical hardships, the abuse and criticism he suffered, and his extended travel (it is estimated that he travelled ten thousand miles during his ministry), he never gave up. He constantly encouraged people to live life to the fullest and to become more like Christ. Isn't that what you yearn for as a Christian? The Apostle went through many trials in his life. Before founding the house-based church in Thessalonica, he founded the Christian church in Philippi. His work was marked by conflict and persecution. "According to his testimony, he was shamelessly mistreated (1 Thess. 2:2)." Luke describes, in the book of Acts, the abuse that Paul suffered. "He is seized, dragged into the marketplace, accused of crimes, publicly beaten with rods, and incarcerated, with his feet fastened in stocks (Acts 16:19-40)."[18] After a stay of an uncertain time, he left Philippi and departed for the city of Thessalonica, a city some one hundred miles to the west, where he established a congregation.[19] Paul did not stay there long, and a painful separation took place (1 Thess. 2:2). In his efforts to keep in touch with the church, he sent Timothy with a letter that encouraged believers not to give up. He encouraged the beleaguered church to persist in their new life despite the fact that members might find it difficult to see the power of God in their lives.

Can you see the power of God at work in your life?

Millions of people in North America have given up on the institutional church, yet many still enjoy a spiritual life

18 See *The Anchor Bible Dictionary*, V, 318.
19 *Ibid*.

and seek answers to spiritual matters. This reminds me of an interesting conversation I had with a teenager recently. He asked, "How can there be a God who created the whole universe yet cares for me individually?" I could understand his question. Here we are in a universe with millions of galaxies – our Milky Way being just one of them. It takes light, travelling at 186,000 miles per second, 160,000 years to go from one end of our galaxy to the other! The nearest galaxy, Andromeda, is 2.9 million light years away.

Andromeda Galaxy

This teen went on to say, "I don't really believe in that God and I don't really need God in my life to do what I do."

I knew that answering his question with the words "have faith" would fall short. What does faith mean in a world where in a matter of weeks massive wealth disappears in stock market crashes or investment scams, a world where war is rampant, hunger is the norm for a majority of the world's poor, AIDS is unstoppable, and resources are shrinking?

And yet, as Paul shows us, faith is the answer. In the face of such questions Paul points to the love of God made known in the person of Jesus Christ. He explains his understanding of what it takes for a Christian community to grow and prosper. He explains his understanding of salvation through belief in Jesus Christ.

Paul believes that there are forces of good and forces of evil in the world and "God's redemption or salvation of believers from sin's enslaving powers and death's corruption is a process that begins with God's free offering of grace (Rom. 5:15)."[20]

For Paul this offer of grace – this creation of a new sphere of existence – does not depend on any previous entitlement, class or social status, or human performance. It depends on faith alone! "Therefore, since we are justified by faith, we have peace with God through our Lord Jesus Christ" (Rom. 5:1). Paul established churches and wrote letters that showed his profound love for them. His words of thanksgiving are often aimed at God in gratitude for the evidence of faith and fruitfulness in the lives of believers. Paul's goal for believers is not "a good life" but "a life that is good" – in other words, a life that truly provides meaning.[21] Paul often writes about his constant concern for the spiritual growth of churches and their members. Paul commends not just their work but also their work in faith; not just their steadfastness but also their steadfastness of hope in the Lord Jesus Christ.[22] Toward the end of his first letter to the Thessalonians he urges people to "encourage one another and build up each other, as indeed you are doing" (1 Thess. 5:11).

This love that Paul writes about and displays is the secret to church growth and to personal growth. It flows from Jesus and his words, "Just as I have loved you, you also should love one another" (Jn. 13:34; see also 15:12,17).

In the present chapter's reading from Romans, Paul reminds us that God is with us at all times – that even while we still were sinners, Christ died for us. Paul knows that

---

20 *The New Interpreter's Bible*, XI, 679.
21 *Ibid.*, 690.
22 *Ibid.*

life brings suffering. He connects suffering with endurance, endurance with character, and character with hope.

You may believe that you are unworthy and therefore not worthy of God's love, but nothing could be further from the truth! Hold fast to God's promises made known to you through the ages. You are a precious child of God. "God's love has been poured into our hearts through the Holy Spirit that has been given to us" (Rom. 5:5). To repeat, God proves his love for us while we still were sinners, Christ died for us.

Don't give up.

Paul tells us to be ready and to be strong in our faith. No one knows the time or the hour when Jesus will return, or for that matter when our time to die will come. Paul encourages believers to live in the light with faith and love and to bear the hope of salvation, because God has destined us to obtain salvation through the Lord Jesus Christ.

CLOSING REFLECTIONS

Denise was a single divorced mother who for years struggled with her faith. In addition, she battled cancer in her adult life. Through it all she never gave up her quest for meaning in life nor her desire to make sense out of life's big questions.

Denise had drifted away from her Methodist church in New England but had never given up on church as a place where she would find the answers she sought. Through the patient guidance of her minister, she returned to the church and immersed herself in small group ministries and Bible studies. She grew in faith and became a beacon of hope to those around her.

Denise lost her battle with cancer yet she has left us with a powerful legacy. Her advice to us is simple yet profound: Never give up; persevere in all matters; God is good! Denise discovered the promise that God would be with her in all circumstances.

Can you relate to Denise's story? How?

Why is there suffering in this world?

Is it possible for God to suffer? If so, how? If not, why not? (For those wishing to read about the suffering of God, I would highly recommend the book The Crucified God: The Cross of Christ as the Foundation and Criticism of Christian Theology *by Jürgen Moltmann.)*

How can you help someone who is suffering from stress or depression? (If you find that life is "too much" and you want to "give up," please reach out for help. Help is there for you!)

3

WHERE IS YOUR HEART?

Romans 6:1-11

Romans 6:1-11

¹What then are we to say? Should we continue in sin in order that grace may abound? ²By no means! How can we who died to sin go on living in it? ³Do you not know that all of us who have been baptized into Christ Jesus were baptized into his death? ⁴Therefore we have been buried with him by baptism into death, so that, just as Christ was raised from the dead by the glory of the Father, so we too might walk in newness of life. ⁵For if we have been united with him in a death like his, we will certainly be united with him in a resurrection like his. ⁶We know that our old self was crucified with him so that the body of sin might be destroyed, and we might no longer be enslaved to sin. ⁷For whoever has died is freed from sin. ⁸But if we have died with Christ, we believe that we will also live with him. ⁹We know that Christ, being raised from the dead, will never die again; death no longer has dominion over him. ¹⁰The death he died, he died to sin, once for all; but the life he lives, he lives to God. ¹¹So you also must consider yourselves dead to sin and alive to God in Christ Jesus.

GOD'S PROMISE

God will give you new and abundant life in Christ.

ROMANS 6:11

FOCUS

The death of the Messiah and the love of God.

THEOLOGICAL BACKGROUND

In his book *Journey to Wholeness: Healing Body, Mind, and Soul,* Thomas Maddix, a member of the Brothers of Holy Cross, shares the story of a friend's struggle with loneliness over a twenty-year period. During that time his friend's suffering increased to the point that she felt "her very being was dying." She yearned for "newness of life."[23]

The pressures of life can take us to desperate places. We all yearn for a newness of life.

Although Paul speaks of sin in this chapter's passage (Rom. 6:1, 2, 6, 7, 10, 11), his ultimate concern for those who hear his voice and read his words is "newness of life." He writes, "... Christ was raised from the dead by the glory of the Father so we too might walk in newness of life" (Rom. 6:4). Paul's earlier letter to the church in Corinth also spoke about "newness of life," connecting the beginning of new life to their becoming Christians. "What this means is that those who become Christians become new persons. They are not the same any more. For the old life is gone. A new life has begun! All this newness of life is from God, who brought us back to himself through what Christ did" (2 Cor. 5:17-18).

---

23 Maddix, *Journey to Wholeness,* 15.

Opening Reflections

What do you seek in life?

How will your search bring you newness of life?

What does newness of life mean for you?

*Read 2 Corinthians 5:17-18 and reflect on Paul's
understanding of the newness of life that is promised
to those who become Christian.*

MEDITATION ON THE PROMISE

THE Apostle Paul proclaims that Jesus Christ died and rose again so that sin would no longer have dominion over us (Rom. 6:1). Men and women are to search their hearts to repent of their sin and turn to God's way of true love in this world. Paul knows that perhaps the biggest problem facing believers is believing that Jesus can in fact forgive sin and that through faith in him they will have new life (Rom. 6:6). Paul knows the history of his people, the Hebrew people. He knows that the prophets wrote and preached about the need for people to trust God and address the sin in their hearts.

Before studying the Romans text, consider the connection the Old Testament prophet Jeremiah drew between the heart, sin, and love. He says, "The sin of Judah is written with an iron pen; with a diamond point it is engraved on the tablet of their hearts, and on the horns of their altars" (Jer. 17:1). He speaks of a heartbroken God whose people had abandoned the covenant; who had forsaken God's love for them; who had pursued lives characterized by greed, selfishness, forgetfulness, and the worship of other gods, forgetting the Sabbath and being concerned only for themselves. He points to the heart as the centre of people's sinfulness, the place where both sin and love can reside, and the place for reform. ✓

You may have been asked, "Do you have Jesus in your heart?" or "Do you know God in your heart?" How did you answer? You, like the man in the following anonymously written story, may feel uncomfortable when someone puts you on the spot like that!

One man, scientifically trained, answered in a very matter of fact way. When asked, "Do you know God in your heart," he replied,

"Everyone knows that the heart is nothing more than a big muscle built to circulate blood in the body – it is simply a blood pump."

"Ah, let me ask you a question young man. Being the day after Valentine's Day, can you remember the days of your youth when you first met a young lady that you fancied?"

"Well yes!"

"Did you ever take her for walks on moonlit nights and hold hands?"

"Well yes!"

"Did you ever stop by the side of a lake on such a walk, as you turned to look at the shimmering moon on the water, did you feel warm all over as you held her in your arms?"

"Yes that is true."

And then, did you take her in your arms, look into her eyes, and tell her with all the tenderness of the moment,

"I love you with all of my blood-pump!"

The heart is the centre of our being, the core of our knowing, the seat of our emotions, and the crux of our essence. Wherein lies the heart, so lie our intentions. Wherein lie our intentions, so lie our actions. God asks about the human heart, "... who can understand it?" (Jer. 17:9). Good question! God responds to his own question by saying,

"I the LORD test the mind and search the heart, to give to all according to their ways, according to the fruit of their doings" (Jer. 17:10).

Jeremiah knew what was going on. The people of Israel had strayed from God. They had set up worship shrines to other gods. They had forgotten God's abundant mercies and goodness and looked to their own strength and wisdom for wealth and happiness. They had forsaken God, the creator and sustainer of life. They did not honour the Sabbath. They did not need God!

"Thus says the LORD," the prophet preaches. "Cursed are those who trust in mere mortals and make mere flesh their strength, whose hearts turn away from the LORD" (Jer. 17:5). Jeremiah knew that sin of the people was deeply engraved upon the tablets of their hearts, written, as he puts it, with an iron pen with a diamond point. Remember your school days and the sound of someone's fingernails scraping across a blackboard? Imagine such a pen engraving sin into your innermost being. This sin is deep and not easily changed.

Jeremiah speaks of the human condition. At the beginning of chapter 17 he alludes to people with an endless desire to accumulate wealth and who give up their high calling for sinful ways. At the end of the chapter he describes how such people forget to honour the Sabbath. Nothing has changed today. Do Jeremiah's words not describe millions of North Americans? Do they not chase after wealth, even on the Sabbath? How easy it is to be self-absorbed!

How would you answer the following questions?

What gods do you and your family serve?

Where is your heart?

What is it that you seek in life? Wealth? Status?

In verse 11 Jeremiah proclaims God's scorn for those who accumulate wealth through injustice: "Like the partridge hatching what it did not lay, so are all who amass wealth unjustly; in mid-life it will leave them, and at their end they will prove to be fools."

Paul asks a profound question that goes to the heart of the believer: "How can we who died to sin go on living in it?" (Rom. 6:2). God knows the intent of our hearts by how we live our lives and by what we do with our time. Is your happiness derived from a God-centred focus in your life? Through Jeremiah, God encouraged his people, even though they had strayed and forgotten his love for them. He encouraged them to put their trust in the Lord, promising that "they shall be like a tree planted by water, sending out its roots by the stream. It shall not fear when heat comes, and its leaves shall stay green ..." (Jer. 17:8).

Stephen A. McAllister

Paul writes that "all of us who have been baptized into Christ Jesus were baptized into his death," and that just as "Christ was raised from the dead by the glory of the Father, so we too might walk in newness of life" (Rom. 6:3, 4). How glorious it is to read Paul's words that "our old self was crucified with him so that the body of sin might be destroyed, and we might no longer be enslaved to sin" (Rom. 6:6). This means we are released from the power and bondage of sin! "For whoever has died is freed from sin" (Rom. 6:7). The good news that Paul gives the Romans, and us, is that Christ liberates us from death so that we might have life; "... if we have died with Christ, we believe that we will also live with him" (Rom. 6:8).

Perhaps today is the day that you will accept Jesus Christ into your heart, and believe in him; the day that you too will be like the tree planted by water, sending out its roots by the stream (Jer. 17:7). Jesus says, "Out of the believer's heart shall flow rivers of living water" (Jn. 7:38). Open your heart today to the love of God, through his son, Jesus Christ.

CLOSING REFLECTIONS

Tracey spent her life as a single woman in the downtown of a central Canadian city, where she faithfully attended a liberal Protestant church. Tracey never drew attention to herself. Perhaps it was her speech impediment that held her back. Tracey loved to have one-on-one conversations with people. Her radiant smile and gracious heart made people feel so good as she shared and listened. Besides having a strong faith, she had a keen sense of intuition and was able to help people discern their calling in life.

Tracey's life was a genuine testimony to the love of God. She passed away a few years ago but her memory lives on through those who were blessed to know her. Tracey knew that God promised new and abundant life in Christ.

How did Tracey's faith live out God's promise that we can have new and abundant life in Christ?

Write your thoughts and feelings about the woman described by Thomas Maddix who "yearned for newness of life." Have you ever yearned for newness of life? How so?

How do you compare our society with the one described by the prophet Jeremiah? (Read Jeremiah 17:1-11.)

How congruent are your actions in life with your heart's desires?

Comment on Jeremiah 17:5, "Cursed is he who trusts in man, Who makes mere flesh his strength, And turns his thoughts from the Lord." (Tanakh)

Is it possible that we have died to sin and yet are still living in it? (Rom. 6:1-2)

What would it mean for you to open your heart more fully to God's will for your life?

4

WHO WILL RESCUE ME?

Romans 7:15-25

Romans 7:15-25

[15]I do not understand my own actions. For I do not do what I want, but I do the very thing I hate. [16]Now if I do what I do not want, I agree that the law is good. [17]But in fact it is no longer I that do it, but sin that dwells within me. [18]For I know that nothing good dwells within me, that is, in my flesh. I can will what is right, but I cannot do it. [19]For I do not do the good I want, but the evil I do not want is what I do. [20]Now if I do what I do not want, it is no longer I that do it, but sin that dwells within me. [21]So I find it to be a law that when I want to do what is good, evil lies close at hand. [22]For I delight in the law of God in my inmost self, [23]but I see in my members another law at war with the law of my mind, making me captive to the law of sin that dwells in my members. [24]Wretched man that I am! Who will rescue me from this body of death? [25]Thanks be to God through Jesus Christ our Lord! So then, with my mind I am a slave to the law of God, but with my flesh I am a slave to the law of sin.

GOD'S PROMISE

God will rescue you from sin.

ROMANS 7:24-25

FOCUS

The conflict within us between
the old and new nature.

THEOLOGICAL BACKGROUND

Paul states that we should consider ourselves "dead to sin and alive to God in Christ Jesus" (Rom. 6:11). What is sin? Our sin is overlain with societal prejudices and the burden of guilt for our misdeeds.

In the Old Testament, sin is seen as a power that deceives men and leads them to destruction.[24] For the ancient Greeks, the word had a more generic meaning, that of fault or being a failure. In philosophy and religion, the Greek word αμαρτημα meant guilt or sin.[25] For the writers of the New Testament, the word we translate as sin (αμαρτια) means to depart from righteousness.

What does it mean to be dead to sin as the Old Testament understands sin? It means we are dead to the power that deceives us and leads us to destruction. In other words, we are therefore dead to the power of sin, and thus the power of sin has no effect on our life! If we are alive to God, we are awake, aware, and aligned to God's purposes and plans for our lives. Sin no longer has the power to pull us away from God's life-giving power.

39

---

24 Bauer et al., *A Greek-English Lexicon of the New Testament, and Other Early Christian Literature*, 43.

25 Liddell et al., *A Greek-English Lexicon*, 77. Plato, *Leges*, 660C, al., Aristoteles, *Ethica Nichomachea*, 1148ª3, al., lxx. Gen. 18.20, al., John 8.46, al.

Opening Reflections

What is sin?

In what ways do you sin?

What does the Apostle Paul mean by "being enslaved to sin"?

Meditation on the Promise

PAUL asks, "Who will rescue me?" and answers his question quickly and succinctly with the words, "Thanks be to God through Jesus Christ our Lord." His words imply that Christ himself rescues us from the power of sin (Rom. 7:24-25). In the previous chapter we looked at the concept of "newness of life," achieved through faith in Christ. The Bible tells us that Jesus Christ came into this world so that we may "have life, and have it abundantly" (Jn. 10:10). The Christian faith places great emphasis on the necessity of personal transformation, or conversion, through faith in Christ. As you think about your personal faith development, consider the conversion stories of three men: John Wesley, the founder of Methodism; John Newton, a former slave runner; and the Apostle Paul.

JOHN WESLEY (1703–1791)

John Wesley's conversion did not occur at an altar rail at the close of a sermon. The moment, on May 24, 1738, was a pivotal one for him. The place was an upper room on Aldersgate-street, London, where Wesley went, "very unwillingly," as he later writes, to hear someone read "Luther's preface to the Epistle to the Romans." Wesley describes his experience in his journal:

About quarter before nine, while he was describing the change which God works in the heart through faith in Christ, I felt my heart strangely warmed. I felt I did trust in Christ, Christ alone for salvation; and an assurance was given me, that he had taken away *my* sins, even *mine*, and saved *me* from the law of sin and death.[26]

Christ Church Cathedral, Oxford, the site of John Wesley's ordination.

Who was Martin Luther and what did he write that so affected Wesley's life? Luther (1483–1546) himself had been greatly moved by the writings of the Apostle Paul. Luther began his term as professor of Sacred Theology at the University of Wittenberg, Saxony, in 1515. The following year he gave lectures on Romans. Luther is best known because of his public challenge to the Roman Catholic Church to amend its ways and practices. Luther, parish priest, monk, and university professor protested church practices through his famous Ninety-Five Theses of October 1517. To his surprise, raising his voice against the church sparked a popular uprising, one that would lead to the Reformation and the birth of the Protestant church.[27] The manuscript of Luther's *Commentary on the Epistle to the Romans* was lost for a long time. A "good copy" was only recently discovered in the Vatican Library in Rome.[28]

Luther says in this commentary, "This letter is truly the most important piece in the New Testament. It is purest Gospel. It is well worth a Christian's while not only to

26 Wesley, *The Journal of the Rev. John Wesley*, A. M., I, 102.
27 McManners, *The Oxford Illustrated History of Christianity*, 245.
28 Luther, *Commentary on the Epistle to the Romans*, preface.

memorize it word for word but also to occupy himself with it daily, as though it were the daily bread of the soul."[29]

So here we are today, struggling with the meaning of the text from Romans, nearly five hundred years after Martin Luther wrote his commentary on Romans, some three decades shy of three hundred years since Wesley's conversion, and nearly twenty centuries after the Apostle Paul wrote his very complex letter to the church in Rome. What does Paul say? He says, "I do not understand my own actions. For I do not do what I want, but I do the very thing I hate" (Rom. 7:15). Later in this passage he writes, "So then, with my mind I am a slave to the law of God, but with my flesh I am a slave to the law of sin" (Rom. 7:25). He also asks, "Who will rescue me from this body of death"? and answers his own question with a resounding, "Thanks be to God through Jesus Christ our Lord!" (Rom. 7:24-25)

N.T. Wright describes this text as "dense and dramatic."[30] Indeed it is very difficult for us to understand, partly because, unlike Paul, most of us have never experienced living under the Law of the Torah. This text speaks to the human condition in a timeless way. You may have thought that you are a good person, yet recognized within yourself a propensity to sin. As Paul reminds us, with our mind we seek to serve God, yet in the flesh we are slaves to sin (Rom. 7:25). Perhaps you have committed a sin and now live with the guilt.

43

John Wesley went to the society meeting at Aldersgate-street struggling with his sin and unbelief. This is not possible, you might be thinking. Surely Wesley was not like ordinary people who have these profound struggles. You may be surprised at the depth of his inner struggles with respect to sin and unbelief. Reflecting on his time in

---

29 Luther, *Preface to the Letter of St. Paul to the Romans.*
30 *The New Interpreter's Bible*, X, 550.

Savannah, Georgia (between 1735 and 1738), where he had served as a missionary (and as an ordained clergy), he writes:

> I knew that the law of God was spiritual; I consented to it, that is was good. Yea, I delighted in it, after the inner man. Yet was I carnal, sold under sin. Everyday was I constrained to cry out, "What I do, I allow not; for what I would, I do not; but what I hate, that I do .... I find a law, that when I would do good, evil is present with me; even the law in my members, warring against the law of my mind, and still bringing me into captivity to the law of sin."

Wesley describes himself "in this vile, abject state of bondage to sin," where, he says, "I was indeed fighting continually, but not conquering."[31] Wesley had returned to England from Georgia in January 1738. He writes, "being in imminent danger of death, and very uneasy on that account, I was strongly convinced that the cause of that uneasiness was unbelief, and that the gaining of a true, living faith, was the one thing needful for me."[32]

Hearing from Luther's commentary changed Wesley's life, and he in turn was largely responsible for the movement of renewal within the Church of England that led to the founding of the Methodist movement, later to become the Methodist Church. Wesley was also one of the spiritual fathers of the holiness / Pentecostal movement.

JOHN NEWTON (1725–1807)

A former slave runner named John Newton wrote the words to the beautiful hymn "Amazing Grace." This hymn has brought comfort to millions of people because it speaks

---

31 Wesley, *The Journal of the Rev. John Wesley, A.M.*, I, 99.
32 *Ibid.*, 100.

of God's love and grace even to those who have sinned – and sinned greatly.

Newton was aboard the slave-ship the *Greyhound* when it encountered a powerful North Atlantic storm. The storm lasted for over a week. The ship's canvas sails ripped and the wood on one side of the ship separated and splintered. The sailors had little hope of survival but mechanically worked the pumps to keep the vessel afloat. On the eleventh day of the storm, sailor Newton was too exhausted to pump, so he was tied to the helm to hold the ship to its course. He was at the helm from one o'clock until midnight. As the storm raged, he had time to think. He saw that his life was as ruined and wrecked as the battered ship he was trying to steer through the storm. The words of Proverbs came to his mind, confirming him in his despair:

Because I have called and you refused, have stretched out my hand and no one heeded, and because you have ignored all my counsel and would have none of my reproof, I also will laugh at your calamity; I will mock when panic strikes you, when panic strikes you like a storm, and your calamity comes like a whirlwind, when distress and anguish come upon you. Then they will call upon me, but I will not answer; they will seek me diligently, but will not find me. Because they hated knowledge and did not choose the fear of the LORD, would have none of my counsel, and despised all my reproof, therefore they shall eat the fruit of their way and be sated with their own devices. (Prov. 1:24-31)

Newton had rejected his mother's teachings and had led other sailors into unbelief. Surely these verses of scripture meant he was beyond hope and beyond saving, yet his thoughts began to turn to Christ. He later found a New

Testament and began to read and he was assured that God might still hear him. He read, "If you then, who are evil, know how to give good gifts to your children, how much more will your Father in heaven give good things to those who ask him!" (Mt. 7:11)

Newton later left slave trading. He became a tide surveyor at Liverpool but began to think he had been called to the ministry. His mother's prayers for her son were answered. In 1764, at the age of thirty-nine, he began forty-three years of preaching the Gospel of Christ. Newton often composed a hymn for Sunday-evening services that developed the lessons and scripture for the evening. Two hundred and eighty of these were collected and combined with sixty-eight hymns by Newton's friend and parishioner William Cowper. They were published in 1779 as the *Olney Hymns*. The most famous of all them, "Faith's Review and Expectation," grew out of King David's exclamation in I Chronicles 17:16-17. We know the hymn today as "Amazing Grace."[33]

Newton continued to preach and have an active ministry until beset by fading health in the last two or three years of his life. He died at the age of eighty-two. Even in those days of ill health, he never ceased to be amazed by God's grace. In the year of his death, he told his friends, "My memory is nearly gone; but I remember two things: That I am a great sinner, and that Christ is a great Savior."[34]

---

33 1 Chron. 17:16-17. The passage reads:
Then King David went in and sat before the LORD, and said, "Who am I, O LORD God, and what is my house, that you have brought me thus far? And even this was a small thing in your sight, O God; you have also spoken of your servant's house for a great while to come. You regard me as someone of high rank, O LORD God!"

34 Wilson, "Amazing Grace: The Story of John Newton, Author of America's Favorite Hymn."

THE APOSTLE PAUL

There is no doubt that Paul would see himself in the words of "Amazing Grace" because he also was blinded, both physically and spiritually and he also, by God's grace, lived to see and to turn his life around and serve God in powerful ways. As Luke tells us in Acts 8:3, Saul (Paul's original Jewish name) ravaged "the church by entering house after house, dragging off both men and women" and committing them "to prison."[35] In Acts 9:1 Luke describes him as "breathing threats and murder against the disciples of the Lord."

Paul was blind to God's grace. He was blind to the pain he caused in people's lives. During this period of his life, he was blinded by his own agenda. Through his focus on the Law and rules, he hurt, persecuted, imprisoned, and even murdered God-fearing people who were simply following:

The King of kings (1 Tim. 6:15)

The Lamb of God (Jn. 1:29)

The Lord of lords (1 Tim. 6:15)

The Son of Man (Jn. 13:31)

Our Savior (2 Tim. 1:10)

Our hope (1 Tim. 1:1)

The one who died for our sins (1 Cor. 15:3).

But God intervened! The story is told in scripture in Acts 9:1-4:

Meanwhile Saul, still breathing threats and murder against the disciples of the Lord, went to the high

---

35 See *Anchor Bible Dictionary*, V, 187, "Commentary on Paul's Jewish ancestry."

priest and asked him for letters to the synagogues at Damascus, so that if he found any who belonged to the Way, men or women, he might bring them bound to Jerusalem. Now as he was going along and approaching Damascus, suddenly a light from heaven flashed around him. He fell to the ground and heard a voice saying to him, "Saul, Saul, why do you persecute me?"

Luke goes on to say:

Saul got up from the ground, and though his eyes were open, he could see nothing; so they led him by the hand and brought him into Damascus. (Acts 9:8)

Luke tells the story of a disciple in Damascus, Ananias, being directed by God in a vision to go and see Saul.

So Ananias went and entered the house. He laid his hands on Saul and said, "Brother Saul, the Lord Jesus, who appeared to you on your way here, has sent me so that you may regain your sight and be filled with the Holy Spirit." (Acts 9:17)

God had another plan for Saul, converting him in an instant on the road to Damascus, taking his sight, and then opening his eyes to see the errors of his ways, his sinful past. Paul regained his sight, both physical and spiritual, and was filled by the Holy Spirit. He devoted the rest of his life to teaching about Jesus the Messiah.

❧

All three of these men experienced conversion in a profound and unexpected manner. God took the most unlikely the murderer (Saul), the slave trader (John Newton), and the sinner (John Wesley) – and in his great mercy used them in powerful ways. If God can do this for these men, imagine what he can do in your life!

John Wesley's statue at Wesley's Chapel, London.

We can take courage from Paul's words, as he proclaims our rescue from the law of sin and of death (Rom. 7:24; 8:2), "Thanks be to God through Jesus Christ our Lord!" (Rom. 7:25)

CLOSING REFLECTIONS

As a young man living in western Canada, Edward spent most of his time with friends whose main purpose in life was to feed their drug habit. It took a lot of money, a lot of time, and a lot of crime to buy these "heavy drugs." As he and his friends were surfing the television one day, they came upon a station broadcasting a church service. They couldn't believe their luck. Here was the answer. These people had money and gladly placed it in the collection plate. It would be simple to go to the church and steal the collection. The following Sunday they put their plan into action. Edward took a gun just in case he needed it.

During the sermon, a miracle occurred. The minister's words pricked Edward's heart. During the altar call, he went forward, placed his gun on the altar, knelt in prayer, and asked God for forgiveness. The church embraced the young man and put his experience and skills to use by having him mentor young people in its drug awareness programs. Eventually, the church sponsored Edward in a Master of Divinity program. He now works with the congregation full-time as an ordained minister.

Edward knows God's promise that he will release us from the power of sin through faith in Christ. His story is an amazing testimony to the power of the Word to transform lives.

Think about Edward's faith journey and reflect on several areas of faith:

Sin
Forgiveness
Reconciliation
Ministry

If God can take a murderer and slave trader to bring his kingdom to so many, what can he do in your life?

What has God already done in your life?

Name a time in your life when you did not understand your own actions. (Rom 7:15)

How does Paul expect Christ to rescue you from the power of sin?

What can you learn about your own spiritual struggles from the story of John Newton's conversion?

5

JESUS, MY JOY

Romans 8:1-11

Romans 8:1-11

¹There is therefore now no condemnation for those who are in Christ Jesus. ²For the law of the Spirit of life in Christ Jesus has set you free from the law of sin and of death. ³For God has done what the law, weakened by the flesh, could not do: by sending his own Son in the likeness of sinful flesh, and to deal with sin, he condemned sin in the flesh, ⁴so that the just requirement of the law might be fulfilled in us, who walk not according to the flesh but according to the Spirit. ⁵For those who live according to the flesh set their minds on the things of the flesh, but those who live according to the Spirit set their minds on the things of the Spirit. ⁶To set the mind on the flesh is death, but to set the mind on the Spirit is life and peace. ⁷For this reason the mind that is set on the flesh is hostile to God; it does not submit to God's law – indeed it cannot, ⁸and those who are in the flesh cannot please God. ⁹But you are not in the flesh; you are in the Spirit, since the Spirit of God dwells in you. Anyone who does not have the Spirit of Christ does not belong to him. ¹⁰But if Christ is in you, though the body is dead because of sin, the Spirit is life because of righteousness. ¹¹If the Spirit of him who raised Jesus from the dead dwells in you, he who raised Christ from the dead will give life to your mortal bodies also through his Spirit that dwells in you.

GOD'S PROMISE

God will restore your life
through the Holy Spirit.

ROMANS 8:11

FOCUS

Life transformed by the Word of God and
the presence of the Holy Spirit.

THEOLOGICAL BACKGROUND

There are numerous references in the New Testament to
the Holy Spirit. One of them is particularly worth some
examination. In Acts 19:2 we are told that when Paul came
to Ephesus, he asked the small band of disciples he found
there, "Did you receive the Holy Spirit when you became
believers?" They replied, "No, we have not even heard that
there is a Holy Spirit." How many of us today struggle to
understand the concept of the Trinity: the Father, Son, and
Holy Spirit?

Desiree LaBine

55

Paul speaks extensively about the Holy Spirit through-out his epistles.[36] David Coffey writes in his wonderful study on the Holy Spirit, "Implicit in this Pauline theology is the understanding that the role of the Holy Spirit as bestowed by the Father on believers, both individually and communally, is to unite them in a mystical manner to the risen Lord, so that from then on they exist and live 'in Christ.' "[37] He adds, "The most basic, even if not the most adequate, statement that can be made about the Holy Spirit is that he is the love with which the Father loves the Son."[38]

I can suggest two additional resources for those who wish to further explore the subject of the Holy Spirit. The first is a major work by renowned Catholic Theologian Yves Congar entitled *I Believe in the Holy Spirit*. This extensive work is divided into three volumes: The Holy Spirit in the Economy: Revelation and Experience of the Spirit; He Is Lord and Giver of Life; and The River of the Water of Life Flows in the East and the West. The second resource is a practical one for preachers by the Senior Minister Emeritus of Riverside Church in New York City, the Rev. Dr. James A. Forbes, Jr. The book is is entitled *The Holy Spirit and Preaching*. I was privileged to hear Dr. Forbes preach at the Lutheran School of Theology in Chicago. I highly recommend his book.

---

36 Passages on the Holy Spirit in Romans alone include: "God's love has been poured into our hearts through the Holy Spirit that has been given to us" (5:5); "My conscience confirms it by the Holy Spirit" (9:1); "For the kingdom of God is ... righteousness and peace and joy in the Holy Spirit" (14:17); "May the God of hope fill you with all joy and peace in believing, so that you may abound in hope by the power of the Holy Spirit" (15:13).
37 Coffey, *Did You Receive the Holy Spirit When You Believed?*, 79.
38 *Ibid.*, 98.

OPENING REFLECTIONS

Consider how "the Spirit of him who raised Jesus from the dead dwells" in us (Rom. 8:11). What does this mean to you?

How do you answer Paul's question in Acts 19:2? Did you receive the Holy Spirit when you became a believer?

MEDITATION ON THE PROMISE

IN the previous chapter we looked at how we can be caught in the power of sin, doing the evil we do not want instead of the good we want (Rom. 7:19). In this chapter I want to consider the power in God's Word that can change our lives and change the world. God's Word has the power to enter your heart and bring to life what God created in you when you were born.

We can grasp what this power is by seeing how the words of scripture influenced the life and work of the poet Johann Franck (1618–1677), the poet and musician Johann Crüger (1598–1662), and the famous composer Johann Sebastian Bach (1685–1750). Their life stories come together in Bach's creation of his beautiful motet, *Jesu, meine Freude* (*Jesus, My Joy*).

Johann Franck was a German poet, lawyer, and public official. He had a religious spirit and a love of nature, writing both secular and religious poetry. He published his first work, *Hundertönige Vaterunsersharfe*, at Guben in 1646. Almost half of his hymn texts are paraphrases of Old Testament Psalms and a few are still found in Protestant hymnals today. Bach composed fourteen settings of seven of Franck's texts, the most famous being the motet *Jesu, meine Freude*, BWV 227.[39]

Johann Crüger began studying theology in Wittenberg in 1620. He received a thorough musical training under Paulus Homberger in Regensburg and was a pupil of Giovanni Gabrieli. Crüger was appointed cantor and organist of the Nikolaikirche (St. Nikolai Church) in Berlin

---

39 Marshall, "Johann Franck (Hymn-Writer)," www.bach-cantatas.com

in 1622, a post he retained till his death. He was one of the most distinguished composers of his time. He composed sacred works for choral and instrumental performances and was a musicologist, writing about the theory and practice of music. His claim to fame, however, is the fact that he composed the melody that Bach used in his motet. The melody first appeared in Crüger's *Praxis Pietatis Melica – 1644*, a collection of hymns for the German Lutheran Church.[40]

Johann Sebastian Bach was the son of Johann Ambrosius Bach, organist and town musician.[41] J.S. Bach was orphaned at the age of ten and went to live with his elder brother, Johann Christoph, at Ohrdruf, where he took klavier and organ lessons. Most musicians regard Bach as one of the greatest geniuses of Western music. He was prolific, writing at least one cantata for every Sunday of the year. There are over a thousand known compositions. Bach's eyesight began to deteriorate during his last year, and the operations and the treatment that followed them may have hastened his death. He took final communion on July 22, 1750, and died six days later. On July 31 he was buried at St John's cemetery. His widow survived him for ten years, dying in poverty in 1760.

In the midst of his first season at Leipzig, while having to produce a cantata for each Sunday of the year, Bach was asked to provide music for the funeral of a distinguished university professor. The result was his longest and most ambitious motet, *Jesu, meine Freude*.

Bach's compositions languished in obscurity for almost eighty years after his death, until Mendelssohn revived his *St. Matthew's Passion* in 1829. Bach's legacy lives on

---

40 Oron, "Johann Crüger (Hymn-Writer, Composer)," www.bach-cantatas. com

41 J.S. Bach, b. March 31, 1685; d. July 18, 1750; organist and composer.

forever in his music. We are blessed to receive both the word and the music! God's Word, transmitted through Paul's Epistle to the Romans, transformed Bach's very being and inspired his music. I include excerpts from the German and English text of the motet to highlight the connection to the Romans text.[42]

Jesus, my joy, pasture of my heart, … apart from you on the earth there is nothing dearer to me.	Jesu, meine Freude, Meines Herzens Weide, … Ausßer dir soll mir auf Erden nichts sonst Liebers werden.
Beneath your protection, I am free from the attacks of all my enemies. Let Satan track me down, … Even if there is thunder and lightning, even if sin and hell spread terror, Jesus will protect me.	Unter deinem Schairmen, bin ich vor den Stürmen, Aller Feinde frei. Laß den Satan wittern, … Ob es itzt gleich kracht und blitzt, ob gleich Sünd und Hölle schrecken: Jesus will mich decken.
Misery, distress, affliction, disgrace and death, even if I must endure much suffering, will not separate me from Jesus,	Elend, Not, Kreuz, Schmach und Tod Soll mich, ob ich viel muss leiden, Nicht von Jesu scheiden,
sinful existence [life of wickedness and depravity],[43] I bid you good night.	du Lasterleben, Gute Nacht gegeben.
Even if here I must endure shame and disgrace, even in suffering you remain, Jesus, my joy!	Duld ich schon hier Spott und Hohn, Dennoch bleibst du auch im Leide, Jesu, meine Freude!

---

42 Browne, transl., *Jesu, meine Freude* (2008).
43 *Cassell's German-English, English-German Dictionary*, 383.

"Jesu, meine Freude" may be translated as "Jesus my joy, my gladness, my delight, my pleasure."[44]

Paul reminds us, "If the Spirit of him who raised Jesus from the dead dwells in you, he who raised Christ from the dead will give life to your mortal bodies also through his Spirit that dwells in you" (Rom. 8:11). In his motet Bach claims that Jesus *is* joy because – in Franck's poetic words, based on Paul's soaring words – Jesus will protect us from all manner of sin, no matter how difficult the situation.

Paul was in many difficult situations. Despite suffering incredible persecution, slander, and resistance, he sought to change the hearts of the people in the churches in Rome, Galatia, Thessalonica, Corinth, Ephesus, and Philippi. What gave him the strength to persevere? The indwelling and power of the Holy Spirit gave Paul the strength to:

Preach like he preached

Speak like he spoke

Write like he wrote

Travel like he travelled

Endure what he endured

Love like he loved and

Name truth for truth's sake.

I invite you to reflect on the genius and beauty of Bach, whose great music was empowered by the simple yet timeless message of the scriptures: God loves you; Christ came into the world so you might have new life through belief in Christ; and you will experience the power of God's Holy Spirit.

---

44 *Ibid.*, 231.

I urge you to pray with the scriptures daily. Take Romans and spend time with the text: study, pray, reflect, and learn. There is a power in God's Word to enter your heart and bring to life what God created in you when you were born. There is power in God's Word to change your life. May the new song of your heart be, Jesus, My Joy!

CLOSING REFLECTIONS

Sister Rosa, whose recent death was mourned by so many, was a member of a religious order in South America. Called to a life of teaching and leadership as head of her religious order, she was revered as a spiritual director, faith mentor, teacher, and community leader. She continued to follow God's call to serve when she immersed herself in the study of the lives of the saints of the Christian faith during her doctoral studies in Rome. Through this rich experience, she became a beacon of life and hope to all she served.

An elderly friend of mine met Sister Rosa during one of her visits to Canada and remarked, "I feel like I met Mother Teresa." Sister Rosa was a living example of the powerful and total transformation that happens when you submit your life to God. She fully experienced God's promise of new and restored life through the presence of Christ, the power of God, and the indwelling of the Holy Spirit.

Paul encourages us to "live according to the Spirit" and "set [our mind] on the things of the Spirit" (Rom. 8:5). How did Sister Rosa do this in her life?

Identify instances in your life in which the "law of the Spirit of life in Christ Jesus set you free from the law of sin and of death." (Rom. 8:2)

Read Galatians 5:14-23. Paul talks there about the fruits of the "flesh" and the fruits of the "Spirit," noting the profound differences in our lives when we choose to live seeking one or the other. How have you experienced these in your church? Why?

What spiritual changes would you like to see in your church? Why?

6

ONLY GOD KNOWS

Romans 8:12-25

Romans 8:12-25

[12]So then, brothers and sisters, we are debtors, not to the flesh, to live according to the flesh – [13]for if you live according to the flesh, you will die; but if by the Spirit you put to death the deeds of the body, you will live. [14]For all who are led by the Spirit of God are children of God. [15]For you did not receive a spirit of slavery to fall back into fear, but you have received a spirit of adoption. When we cry, "Abba! Father!" [16]it is that very Spirit bearing witness with our spirit that we are children of God, [17]and if children, then heirs, heirs of God and joint heirs with Christ – if, in fact, we suffer with him so that we may also be glorified with him. [18]I consider that the sufferings of this present time are not worth comparing with the glory about to be revealed to us. [19]For the creation waits with eager longing for the revealing of the children of God; [20]for the creation was subjected to futility, not of its own will but by the will of the one who subjected it, in hope [21]that the creation itself will be set free from its bondage to decay and will obtain the freedom of the glory of the children of God. [22]We know that the whole creation has been groaning in labor pains until now; [23]and not only the creation, but we ourselves, who have the first fruits of the Spirit, groan inwardly while we wait for adoption, the redemption of our bodies. [24]For in hope we were saved. Now hope that is seen is not hope. For who hopes for what is seen? [25]But if we hope for what we do not see, we wait for it with patience.

GOD'S PROMISE

God promises that the revealed glory
will exceed your present suffering.

ROMANS 8:17

FOCUS

The need to wait in hope with patience and prayer.

THEOLOGICAL BACKGROUND

Dietrich Bonhoeffer was born on February 4, 1906, in Breslau, Germany.[45] Student, teacher, writer, son, theologian, pastor, chaplain, and double agent – all these words describe Bonhoeffer yet do not fully explain him. On April 9, 1945, at the age of thirty-nine, he was executed in a Gestapo prison for his part in a failed attempt to kill Hitler. His death has been heralded as that of a martyr.

Dietrich Bonhoeffer

We owe a great debt to Eberhard Bethge, Bonhoeffer's long-time friend and colleague, for preserving and editing his letters. The following excerpt is taken from a letter

45 Bethge and Barnett, *Dietrich Bonhoeffer*, 3.

Bonhoeffer wrote to Bethge from his cell in the Gestapo prison at Tegel on July 21, 1944, just nine months before his death. It contains Bonhoeffer's profound thoughts on living in faith, even though he knows the hopeless position he is in, incarcerated in the Gestapo prison for his role in the attempted assassination of Hitler. He speaks about faith, humility, and sharing in God's suffering by considering not his own suffering but those of others. I believe that Bonhoeffer was at peace with his participation in the events meant to bring down the Third Reich. He knew that his actions were meant to alleviate the suffering of millions. Bonhoeffer gave himself completely to God. He wrote:

> I discovered later, and I am still discovering right up to this moment, that it is only by living completely in this world that one learns to have faith. One must completely abandon any attempt to make something of oneself, whether it be a saint, or converted sinner, or a churchman (a so-called priestly type!), a righteous man or an unrighteous one, a sick man or a healthy one. By this-worldliness, I mean living unreservedly in life's duties, problems, successes and failures, experiences and perplexities. In so doing, we throw ourselves completely into the arms of God, taking seriously, not our own sufferings, with those of God in the world – watching with Christ in Gethsemane. That, I think, is faith, that is metanoia; and that is how one becomes a man and a Christian (cf. Jer. 45!).[46] How can success make us arrogant, or failure lead us astray, when we share in God's suffering through a life of this kind?[47]

---

46 metanoia, Greek μετανοια: repentance, a change of mind, remorse, turning about, conversion. Bauer et al., *A Greek-English Lexicon of the New Testament, and Other Early Christian Literature*, 512.

47 Bonhoeffer, *Letters and Papers from Prison*, 370.

OPENING REFLECTIONS

It seems that we are always in a hurry. The Apostle Paul says we must wait with patience for hope that we cannot see. How can we understand this in the context of our busy lives?

Reflect on Bonhoeffer's letter. Read about his life and ministry. You may enjoy reading his classic book The Cost of Discipleship, *in which he states:*

Suffering and rejection are laid upon Jesus as a divine neccesity, and every attempt to prevent it is the work of the devil, especially when it comes from his own disciples; for it is in fact an attempt to prevent Christ from being Christ. Peter's protest displays his own unwillingness to suffer, and that means that Satan has gained entry into the Church, and is trying to tear it away from the cross of its Lord.[48]

What do you think of this statement?

---

48 Bonhoeffer, *The Cost of Discipleship*, 87.

MEDITATION ON THE PROMISE

ONCE there was an old man who lived in a tiny village.[49] Although poor, he was envied by all, for he owned a beautiful white horse. Even the king coveted his treasure. A horse like this had never been seen before – such was its splendor, its majesty, and its strength.

People offered fabulous prices for the steed, but the old man always refused. "This horse is not a horse to me," he would tell them. "It is like a person, a friend. How could you sell a friend? He is a friend, not a possession." The man was poor and the temptation was great. But he never sold the horse.

One morning he found that the horse was not in the stable. The entire village came to see him. "You old fool," they scoffed, "we told you that someone would steal your horse. We warned you that you would be robbed. You are so poor. How could you ever hope to protect such a valuable animal? It would have been better to sell him. You could have gotten whatever price you wanted. No amount would have been too high. Now the horse is gone, and you've been cursed with misfortune."

The old man responded, "Don't speak too quickly. Say only that the horse is not in the stable. That is all we know; the rest is judgment. If I've been cursed or not, how can you know? How can you judge?"

The people contested, "Don't make us out to be fools! We may not be philosophers, but great philosophy is not needed. The simple fact is that your horse is gone is a curse."

70

49 This story is reprinted by permission. *In the Eye of the Storm*, Max Lucado, copyright 1991, Thomas Nelson Inc. Nashville, Tennessee. All rights reserved.

The old man spoke again. "All I know is that the stable is empty, and the horse is gone. The rest I don't know. Whether it is a curse or a blessing, I can't say. All we can see is a fragment. Who can say what will come next?"

> *The old man spoke again. "No one knows if what happens is a blessing or a curse. No one is wise enough to know. Only God knows."*

The people of the village laughed. They thought that the man was crazy. They had always thought he was a fool; if he wasn't, he would have sold the horse and lived off the money. But instead, he was a poor woodcutter, an old man still cutting firewood and dragging it out of the forest and selling it. He lived hand to mouth in the misery of poverty. Now he had proven that he was, indeed, a fool.

After fifteen days, the horse returned. He hadn't been stolen; he had run away into the forest. Not only had he returned, he had brought a dozen wild horses with him. Once again the village people gathered around the woodcutter and spoke. "Old man, you were right and we were wrong. What we thought was a curse was a blessing. Please forgive us."

The man responded, "Once again, you go too far. Say only that the horse is back. State only that a dozen horses returned with him, but don't judge. How do you know if this is a blessing or not? You see only a fragment. Unless you know the whole story, how can you judge? You read only one page of a book. Can you judge the whole book? You read only one word of a phrase. Can you understand the entire phrase?

"Life is so vast, yet you judge all of life with one page or one word. All you have is a fragment! Don't say that this is a blessing. No one knows. I am content with what I know. I am not perturbed by what I don't."

"Maybe the old man is right," they said to one another. So they said little. But down deep, they knew he was wrong. They knew it was a blessing. Twelve wild horses had returned with one horse. With a little bit of work, the animals could be broken and trained and sold for much money.

The old man had a son, an only son. The young man began to break the wild horses. After a few days, he fell from one of the horses and broke both legs. Once again the villagers gathered around the old man and cast their judgments.

"You were right," they said. "You proved you were right. The dozen horses were not a blessing. They were a curse. Your only son has broken his legs, and now in your old age you have no one to help you. Now you are poorer than ever."

The old man spoke again. "You people are obsessed with judging. Don't go so far. Say only that my son broke his legs. Who knows if it is a blessing or a curse? No one knows. We only have a fragment. Life comes in fragments."

It so happened that a few weeks later the country engaged in war against a neighboring country. All the young men of the village were required to join the army. Only the son of the old man was excluded, because he was injured. Once again the people gathered around the old man, crying and screaming because their sons had been taken. There was little chance that they would return. The enemy was strong, and the war would be a losing struggle. They would never see their sons again.

"You were right, old man," they wept. "God knows you were right. This proves it. Your son's accident was a blessing. His legs may be broken, but at least he is with you. Our sons are gone forever."

The old man spoke again. "It is impossible to talk with you. You always draw conclusions. No one knows. Say only this: Your sons had to go to war, and mine did not. No one knows if it is a blessing or a curse. No one is wise enough to know. Only God knows."

Who among us cannot relate in some way to this old man? Things happen to us in life and sometimes too much! We lose our footing, we feel stressed, and we cannot cope. Perhaps we even want to give up. Family, friends, and neighbours may help us when we are down and out, or they may be quick to point out our faults and tell us why what has happened to us is "just what we deserve." The last thing we need when we ask for help is to hear the words, "If you had just listened to me, you wouldn't be calling me – when will you ever learn?"

The villagers were very quick to come by and judge everything that happened to the poor old man. Good, bad, or indifferent, they knew what was happening in his life. They were anxious to share their thoughts with him, even if he didn't need any advice.

This sounds somewhat like the story of Job in the Old Testament. How Job suffered! He suffered the death of loved ones, the loss of home and herds, the loss of health, and the loss of hope. How did Job's friends respond? They came to comfort him and to blame him, saying, "God does not keep the wicked alive, but gives the afflicted their right" (Job 36:6). In other words, Job's friends believed that he deserved what he got. Eventually Job turned his anger toward God and demanded that he explain why all of these bad things happened to such a faithful servant.

Many of us have been there. We respond the same way: Why, oh God, why me – why do my children get hurt;

why does my marriage suffer; why does he say such mean things; why is my best friend so sick; why did she have to die; why did I lose my job; why doesn't she understand; so many questions – why, oh why?

God answers Job's lament out of the whirlwind: "Who is this that darkens counsel by words without knowledge?" (Job 38:2). Job learns that it is God who creates – it is God who nurtures – it is by God's wisdom and grace that "the world and all that is" was created, and it is by God's "wisdom and grace" that we have life. We are born of dust, the spirit of life is blown into us, and when our time is finished, in God's time, our breath fades, and it is to the earth that we return, earth to earth, dust to dust! (Sirach 17:32)

As much as we like to be in control of life and all that happens to us, when we are most unaware or unprepared, life brings us back to the place where all we can do is call out, ABBA – DADDY – GOD – be with me in this time! "Then Job answered the LORD: 'I know that you can do all things, and that no purpose of yours can be thwarted" (Job 42:1-2).

Paul writes to the church in Rome, and in fact to all Christians, saying that we will experience joys and suffering in life. In fact, he goes deeper and says that the road to inheritance, the path to glory, lies alongside the path of suffering. Just as our Lord suffered, we too will experience suffering as we claim and proclaim the gospel message. Dietrich Bonhoeffer (see the Theological Background at the beginning of this chapter) contrasts "cheap grace" and "costly grace" when he writes about the cost of becoming a follower of Jesus Christ:

Cheap grace is the preaching of forgiveness without requiring repentance, baptism without church discipline, communion without confession, absolution without personal confession. Cheap grace is grace without discipleship, grace without the cross, grace without Jesus Christ, living and incarnate. Costly grace is the Word of God which God speaks as it pleases him. Costly grace confronts us as a gracious call to follow Jesus; it comes as a word of forgiveness to the broken spirit and the contrite heart. Grace is costly, because it compels a man to submit to the yoke of Christ and follow him; it is grace, because Jesus says, "my yoke is easy and my burden is light."[50]

If you are a student of church history, you may have read about the suffering endured by Christians in the past. At the Nicene Council, an important church meeting in the fourth century A.D., fewer than twelve of the three hundred and eighteen delegates attending had not lost an eye or a hand or did not limp on a leg lamed by torture for their Christian faith.[51] Things are much better for us today, although many Christians are still persecuted for their faith. What gives Christians the strength to:

Persevere
> *Tell the old, old story*
> *Walk into the slums of Calcutta to bring the good news of Christ*
>> *Go into the darkened prison cells and offer words of hope to the hopeless*
> *Visit the sick*
>> *Feed the hungry*
Clothe the homeless and
> *Pray for the lost?*

---

50 Bonhoeffer, *The Cost of Discipleship*, 45.
51 scribd.com, "Steadfast Faithfulness."

Part of the glory, Paul says, consists of being God's agents in bringing healing and restorative divine justice to the whole created order. This means bringing healing and justice to a world in pain, to people who need hope, and to people seeking the promise of eternal salvation. In this way we follow the example of Jesus who gave new life and hope to the poor, the afflicted, the contrite, the brokenhearted, the unimportant, and the unpretentious. Remember, it was the religious elite, the scholars, and the pious folk who rejected Christ and his teachings.

The old man with the horse took life in stride, trusting in God. He did not blame God for what happened. He knew that God was with him through all that happened. His story speaks of a way of being that is more circumspect and patient in living: "Life is so vast," he says, "yet you judge all of life with one page or one word. All you have is a fragment! God gives us one day at a time. The past is gone, tomorrow but a dream!"

The present groaning is a sign, Paul says: a sign not of a fully redeemed state but of the Christian's sure and certain hope. We will not live in this state forever. We are saved in hope, which means that our future salvation is not yet visible.

How should we wait? How should we live? Paul tells us to wait with patience and prayer. Patience and prayer are the appropriate stance and activity for God's people while awaiting final redemption. As faith-filled Christians, let us turn our thoughts and minds to a life of patience and prayer, aware that in God's time and in God's way, all will be revealed, that in the fullness of time we will find the path to glory and receive the eternal inheritance of our salvation.

The Apostle Paul reminds us to consider that "the sufferings of this present time are not worth comparing with the glory about to be revealed to us" (Rom. 8:18), "for in hope we were saved. Now hope that is seen is not hope. For who hopes for what is seen? But if we hope for what we do not see, we wait for it with patience" (Rom. 8:24-25).

CLOSING REFLECTIONS

Sister Latoya grew up in a small village in East Africa. One of eight children, she followed her older sister into the convent where she studied and worked to become a nun. After her novitiate, Latoya spent twelve years in ministry to the poor and the destitute, never giving thought to her own needs but always seeking to do God's will in very trying circumstances. After that time she made her life profession to serve God.

Sister Latoya was later sent to the United States to undertake specialized studies in pastoral care and has since returned to her ministry of pastoral care and spiritual formation with her community in East Africa. She is a wonderful servant of God who knows from personal experience that the revealed glory will far exceed the present suffering.

Reflect on Sister Latoya's life and share your thoughts
about her spiritual journey, her life of Christian service, and the suffering she may have either endured or witnessed as she lived out her calling.

How can you relate to the old man's story as shared by Max Lucado?

What does it mean to live by the Spirit?

Paul says that the tension between suffering and hope in the glory to come (Rom. 5:3-5) is characteristic of the Christian life in this present time (Rom. 8:18). What do you think of this belief? Why?

What does it mean to hope for what we have not seen for as Paul says, "in hope we were saved" (Rom. 8:24)? Do you believe this? Why or why not?

What does Paul mean by "all will be revealed"? (Rom. 8:18)

Why is there suffering? How have you suffered for the gospel?

7

COMPLACENCY OR COMMITMENT?

Romans 9:1-5

Romans 9:1-5

¹I am speaking the truth in Christ – I am not lying; my conscience confirms it by the Holy Spirit – ²I have great sorrow and unceasing anguish in my heart. ³For I could wish that I myself were accursed and cut off from Christ for the sake of my own people, my kindred according to the flesh. ⁴They are Israelites, and to them belong the adoption, the glory, the covenants, the giving of the law, the worship, and the promises; ⁵to them belong the patriarchs, and from them, according to the flesh, comes the Messiah, who is over all, God blessed forever. Amen.

GOD'S PROMISE

The Messiah is over all.

ROMANS 9:5

FOCUS

Paul's distress over the degree of
unbelief of his own people.

THEOLOGICAL BACKGROUND

When Peter addressed the crowd on the day of Pentecost,
he told them, "You are the descendants of the prophets and
of the covenant that God gave to your ancestors, saying
to Abraham, 'And in your descendants all the families of
the earth shall be blessed' " (Acts 3:25). Referring to God's
promise to send the Messiah, the Apostle Paul writes,
"And this is my covenant with them, when I take away
their sins" (Rom. 11:27).

What does the word *covenant* mean? Turn to the book
of Genesis in the Old Testament and read the account of
God's promise and covenant with Abraham (Gen. 15). The
scholar Gerhard von Rad says that "belief alone has brought
Abraham into a proper relationship to God."[52] God gives
no answers to Abram's doubting questions. Instead, God
enters into a covenant with Abram based on the ancient
tradition of walking between the cut halves of an animal
(hence the phrase "to cut a contract"). "Abraham sees God
himself passing through the pieces, thereby emphasizing
that the divine promise is secure."[53]

What is powerful about this covenant is that God
himself is pledging to honour it (Gen. 15:17). This is an

---

52 Rad, *Genesis*, 185
53 "Gleanings" comment on Gen. 15:10 in *The Torah*, 113.

unconditional promise by God with Abram as a witness. It is interesting that during this time Abram had fallen into a deep sleep, a time when the activities of the mind and spirit are extinguished, but when man is awake to revelation. God tells Abram that he will die in peace in his old age; he will not live to see the covenant fulfilled.

OPENING REFLECTIONS

Read the stories of Abram and Sarai and reflect on the powerful intertwining of the concepts of promise, blessing, and covenant (Gen. 15, 16).

What are the signs of spiritual commitment or complacency in your life?

What new commitment can you make today to turn your life back to God and God's purpose for you?

MEDITATION ON THE PROMISE

A few years ago, my wife Susan and I helped my father prepare to sell his home. We had to pack all his belongings. It involved sorting, discarding, giving away, throwing away, and then organizing and moving the remainder. It was amazing to see the transformation as we emptied the house: one day full and days later empty.

Desiree LaBine

Recently Susan showed me a book that my father gave her at the time of the move, Pierre Berton's *The Comfortable Pew*.[54] Inside the front cover were the signatures of sixteen people who attended a study group on the book at my father's church, including my grandmother and mother, both since deceased. It was quite a surprise to see the list; it brought back so many memories. In its day the book was a record Canadian bestseller with upward of 200,000 copies sold. It provoked hundreds of editorials and reviews and thousands of people read it in study groups.[55]

---

54 Berton, *The Comfortable Pew*.
55 Creal, "The Comfortable Pew Revisited."

The Anglican Church had retained Berton in 1963 to take a critical look at Christianity and the religious establishment of the new age. Before beginning the assignment, Berton asked that the research cover all major Christian denominations in Canada, and his wish was granted. For some readers his findings were interesting; for many they were refreshing; yet for others the results were threatening. Although Berton's book received a wide readership, it also attracted much criticism from the church as it defended itself. Here are some of his findings:

Worship

Many of the people who call themselves Christian say: the liturgy is "dull and old fashioned," the phraseology unfamiliar, the words archaic, the organ music "square," the congregation spiritless.[56]

There are some who say (nearly always in private) that they would quite like to go to church or chapel but they feel absolutely bored or appreciably embarrassed by what goes on inside.[57]

The church's concerns over bun-fights, budgets, organizations, and tea drinking with parishioners and finding new ways to get people into the church and raise contributions was overshadowing its true work.[58]

Though Christ clearly intended the opposite, churchgoing appears to put more emphasis on formalized religious observance than it does on ethical relationships.[59]

It has been said that none of the twelve apostles would feel at home in a modern church. Nor is it

---

56 Berton, *The Comfortable Pew*, 104.
57 *Ibid.*, 29.
58 *Ibid.*, 72.
59 *Ibid.*, 85.

likely that a modern church would welcome the kind of people with whom its founder associated.[60]

Clergy

The "divine discontent" that once distinguished the Protestant minister or priest has been replaced by what Mumford calls a "complacent pedestrianism."[61]

What really concerned me was the discovery that the vast mass of ecclesiastics differed in no real sense from the vast mass of laymen. They conformed.[62]

... the failure of the Sunday sermon to communicate the vitality of the Christian message in relevant contemporary terms.[63]

Berton discovered a weakened church. He found that clergy and parishioners were complicit in this situation. Both had become complacent in their actions and in their expectations. He identified "a virus that has been weakening the church for more than a generation."[64] Berton noted that large numbers of nominal Christians were no longer very hot or very cold, for the virus that had weakened the church was apathy. He quotes from the book of Revelation (3:15-16):

> I know your works; you are neither cold nor hot. I wish that you were either cold or hot. So, because you are lukewarm, and neither cold nor hot, I am about to spit you out of my mouth.

Berton was talking about complacency: complacency in the church as a result of the complacency of both clergy and

---

60 *Ibid.*, 90.
61 *Ibid.*, 30.
62 *Ibid.*, 21.
63 *Ibid.*, 131.
64 *Ibid.*, 29.

parishioners. The writer of the book of Revelation was also talking about complacency; of people who were "lukewarm, and neither cold nor hot."[65] Complacency in the hearts of God's people is nothing new. The prophet Zephaniah wrote these words twenty-six centuries ago:

> At that time I will search Jerusalem with lamps, and I will punish the people who rest complacently on their dregs ... (Zeph. 1:12)[66]

Have we have become lazy in our faith life? The Apostle Paul writes in his letter to the Romans about a deeper complacency: a satisfaction with the status quo and an unwillingness to accept the gospel message. The majority of Paul's Jewish contemporaries did not believe in the gospel of Jesus Christ and Paul believed that they were excluded from salvation.[67] To compound the problem, some of the Christian gentiles hoped that the Jews would remain forever in this condition.

Paul is agitated over the question of why other nations are partaking of Israel's heritage through the gospel "while his own kinfolk are missing out on the gospel." How can this anomaly be resolved?[68] Paul must have remembered how his forefathers had turned against God and broken the covenant. Moses came down from the mountain where he received God's commandments for the people and found the people worshipping a golden calf that they had made while waiting for him (Ex. 32:1-6). How did Moses, the Apostle Paul, and Pierre Berton each respond to the crisis of complacency of faith?

---

65 *The New Oxford Annotated Bible*, Rev. 3:13-17.
66 *The Anchor Bible Dictionary*, VI, 1077. Zephaniah is the ninth book of the twelve Minor Prophets, containing the oracles of the prophet Zephaniah. Zephaniah was active during the reign of Josiah (640–609, B.C.E.)
67 *The New Interpreter's Bible*, X, 627.
68 Dunn, *The Theology of Paul the Apostle*, 509.

Moses had two responses: the first was anger and the second was to offer himself as atonement. The scriptures say that Moses' anger "burned hot" (Ex. 32:19).

> [He] threw the stone tablets to the ground, smashing them at the foot of the mountain. He took the calf they had made and burned it. Then he ground it into powder, threw it into the water, and forced the people to drink it. (Ex. 32:19-20)

Moses then commanded the sons of Levi to to kill those who were "running wild" in the camps. "The Levites obeyed Moses' command, and about 3,000 people died that day" (Ex. 32:28).

On the next day Moses said to the people, "You have sinned a great sin. But now I will go up to the Lord; perhaps I can make atonement for your sin" (Ex. 32:30).

Complacency is a blight that saps energy, dulls attitudes, and causes a drain on the brain. The first symptom is satisfaction with things as they are. The second is rejection of things as they might be. "Good enough" becomes today's watchword and tomorrow's standard. Complacency makes people fear the unknown, mistrust the untried, and abhor the new. Like water, complacent people follow the easiest course – downhill. They draw false strength from looking back.

– FROM *BITS AND PIECES*

The Apostle Paul writes to the church in Rome and expressed the "great sorrow and unceasing anguish in [his] heart" (Rom. 9:2).

And as for Berton, what did he recommend in *The*

Comfortable Pew as he discovered such trends? He was not afraid to name what he saw as the solution to bringing the church back to life, that is, bringing the living gospel back into peoples' lives. He wrote:

> These were two ways in which a truly Christian reformation could come about. It could come through some terrifying persecution of the Christian Church – persecution that would rid the Church of those of little faith, of the status seekers and respectability-hunters, of the deadwood who enjoy the club atmosphere, of the ecclesiastical hangers-on, and the comfort seekers. Once the church becomes the most uncomfortable institution in the community, only those who really matter will stick with it. At this point, one would expect that Church to come back to the basic principles of love, faith, and hope that have made martyrs out of men.[69]

You can see why Berton had his critics! I wonder if he was thinking like Moses. This is radical thinking for our time. The reality is that complacency and apathy separate many of our neighbours from the gospel of Christ. Many churches are virtually empty. *Apathy! Complacency! Displacement!* This is not new. John Wesley was very critical of the complacency that had settled into the Church of England, referring to the "dry rot" that had crept into the pulpits of the church.[70]

Denominations in Canada and the United States are suffering declines in membership. The following denominations are listed in the 77th annual edition of *The Yearbook of American & Canadian Churches* as

---

69 Berton, *The Comfortable Pew*, 143.
70 Abraham, *Wesley for Armchair Theologians*, 33.

experiencing the highest rate of membership loss: the United Church of Christ (down 6.01 percent); the African Methodist Episcopal Zion Church (down 3.01 percent); the Presbyterian Church (USA) (down 2.79 percent); the Lutheran Church – Missouri Synod (down 1.44 percent); and the Evangelical Lutheran Church in America (down 1.35 percent).[71] In Europe, the Roman Catholic Cardinal of Vienna, Christoph Cardinal Schönborn, was even more blunt than Berton, stating in 2009 that "Christianity in Europe is coming to an end."[72]

Stephen A. McAllister

Downtown United Church for sale, 2009.

What has happened in Canada since Berton wrote his book? The number of people in Ontario who reported that they had no religion increased 48 percent from 1991 to 2001 to more than 1.8 million persons. The decline within the United Church is significant. The number of people under

71 ekklesia.co.uk, "Southern Baptists and Catholics Join US Church Decline Trend."
72 lifesitenews.com, " 'Christianity in Europe Coming to an End': Vienna Cardinal."

pastoral care in the Toronto Conference decreased from 115,316 in 1980 to 57,542 in 2004. The downward decline continues unabated with no turnaround in sight.[73]

Is there any hope for the declining Christian church? I believe that a new Christian reformation will come about when those who believe the gospel *really believe* and tell people about the exciting and powerful words of the liberating and life-giving message of hope and salvation as modelled and taught by our Lord.

Berton ended his book with his belief that real transformation will come about as the result of the actions of a man (sic) who will

> take all of the incredible laws, postures, and myths of today's church and turn them inside out, so they have some relevance in the New Age. Such a man (sic), seeing through the murky varnish of wealth, snobbery, self-seeking and apathy, which overlays the church, to the essential message at its core, would by sacrifice and total commitment, work his modern miracles. His real communication would be through his own commitment to his faith.[74]

Complacency versus commitment ... the choice is yours. It is time for the church and its members to become more accountable to a life of:

Learning

Prayer

---

73 McAllister, *Revival of Wexford Heights United Church*, 84. The membership in churches in the Toronto Scarborough Presbytery decreased from 10,407 in 1980 to 3,953 in 2004. This represents a compound rate of decline of 3.8 percent per year for the twenty-five year period. I estimate that at the current rate of decline, by the year 2011, there will be approximately 1,800 persons registered on the rolls of United Churches in the Toronto Scarborough Presbytery.

74 Berton, *The Uncomfortable Pew*, 144.

Mission

Mutual respect and love, and

Teaching and witnessing.

The Bible tells us how we should live our faith. We need to be:

Bold in our proclamation (1 Cor. 2:4)
My speech and my proclamation were not with plausible words of wisdom, but with a demonstration of the Spirit and of power ...

Humble in our service (Mt. 23:12)
All who exalt themselves will be humbled, and all who humble themselves will be exalted.

Sincere in our faith (1 Tim. 1:5)
But the aim of such instruction is love that comes from a pure heart, a good conscience, and sincere faith.

Fearful of our God (Prov. 2:5)
... then you will understand the fear of the LORD and find the knowledge of God.

Show kindness to strangers (Heb. 13:2)
Do not neglect to show hospitality to strangers, for by doing that some have entertained angels without knowing it.

Forgive those who wrong you (Lk. 17:4)
And if the same person sins against you seven times a day, and turns back to you seven times and says, "I repent," you must forgive.

Pray unceasingly (Rom. 1:9-10)
For God, whom I serve with my spirit by announcing

the gospel of his Son, is my witness that without ceasing I remember you always in my prayers, asking that by God's will I may somehow at last succeed in coming to you.

And in all things give thanks (Eph. 5:20)
... giving thanks to God the Father at all times and for everything in the name of our Lord Jesus Christ.

APATHY AND COMPLACENCY

The Apostle Paul had great sorrow and unceasing anguish in his heart because of his people's inability to embrace Jesus as the Messiah. How much more must our Lord ache when he sees the apathy and complacency that has gripped our land and infected our churches – when he sees that we too have made our golden calves. Imagine how Moses would feel today?

I believe that complacency may kill the church as we know it, but that the Holy Spirit will appear in new places where the basic principles of love, faith, and hope live, and where the good news of salvation as taught by the Master himself will be preached, heard, and believed!

CLOSING REFLECTIONS

Jacob grew up in a liberal Protestant church environment in central Canada. In his early adult years he moved to an evangelical church, where he and his family now attend. He changed churches for a number of reasons but primarily because his faith was not being fed, and he wanted to worship in an environment where commitment rather than complacency was the norm.

Like John Wesley in his day, Jacob was critical of churches where worship was by rote and people were not engaged in living out their Christian witness. Wesley was critical of those he called half-Christians, lukewarm Christians, saying that they drained him of his strength. He asked to be delivered from half-Christians.[75]

Jacob serves in a number of church leadership roles, has an active prayer and Bible-study life, and can truly say that his life, along with that of his family, has been transformed by God's love. He believes in God's promise that the Messiah is over all!

In what ways have you become complacent in your life, whether...

At home

At work

Socially

At church

---

75 Collins, *A Real Christian*, 37. Wesley writes:
And this, I bless God, I can in some measure, so long as I avoid that bane of piety, the company of good sort of men, lukewarm Christians (as they are called), persons that have a great concern for, but no sense of, religion. But these insensibly undermine all my resolutions, and quite steal from me the little fervor I have; and I never come from among these "saints of the world" ... faint, dissipated, and shorn of all my strength, but I say, "God deliver me from a half-Christian."

What are the signs of spiritual commitment or complacency in your church?

What does it mean to make a commitment in your faith life?

Why or why not is it important in today's society to have a belief in God and in God's saving power made known through Jesus Christ?

8

HOW BEAUTIFUL ARE THE FEET

Romans 10:5-15

Romans 10:5-15

THE SEASON AFTER PENTECOST, YEAR A, PROPER 14

⁵Moses writes concerning the righteousness that comes from the law, that "the person who does these things will live by them." ⁶But the righteousness that comes from faith says, "Do not say in your heart, 'Who will ascend into heaven?' " (that is, to bring Christ down) ⁷"or 'Who will descend into the abyss?' " (that is, to bring Christ up from the dead). ⁸But what does it say? "The word is near you, on your lips and in your heart" (that is, the word of faith that we proclaim); ⁹because if you confess with your lips that Jesus is Lord and believe in your heart that God raised him from the dead, you will be saved. ¹⁰For one believes with the heart and so is justified, and one confesses with the mouth and so is saved. ¹¹The scripture says, "No one who believes in him will be put to shame." ¹²For there is no distinction between Jew and Greek; the same Lord is Lord of all and is generous to all who call on him. ¹³For, "Everyone who calls on the name of the Lord shall be saved." ¹⁴But how are they to call on one in whom they have not believed? And how are they to believe in one of whom they have never heard? And how are they to hear without someone to proclaim him? ¹⁵And how are they to proclaim him unless they are sent? As it is written, "How beautiful are the feet of those who bring good news!"

GOD'S PROMISE

The Good News will be proclaimed!

ROMANS 10:15

FOCUS

The importance of proclamation.

THEOLOGICAL BACKGROUND

This chapter should provide a word of great encouragement for those who are either serving in a ministry of some sort or who are considering a call to service or ministry. You may resist the invitation to serve as Moses did when God said to him, "So come, I will send you to Pharaoh to bring my people, the Israelites, out of Egypt" (Ex. 3:10). It was no small task that God asked Moses to do. This was not a trip to the corner store for a loaf of bread. This was a huge challenge – an incredible undertaking, to release the Israelites from slavery to freedom.

God called Moses to be the agent of salvation for an entire nation, to be the agent of transformation and healing for a broken and hurting world. What an incredible assignment! God did not give Moses a choice. He charged him with "mission impossible." Understandably, Moses did not want the assignment. He asked God, "Who am I that I should go to Pharaoh, and bring the Israelites out of Egypt?" (Ex. 3:11) Moses felt overwhelmed by what God was asking him to do. There are times when we resist that call and like Moses wonder, "Who am I that I should go?"

Have you experienced times in your life when you have wondered about your ability to do something that you know God has called you to do? We all have doubts and fears. I know about resisting God's call. That was part of my call to ministry during the ten years of my journey to ordination. I was a great procrastinator! Many times I wondered how God could be calling me to make such a radical change in my life: to completely rethink my goals and aspirations; to leave behind the world I knew and move forward into unknown and challenging territory. There were times that I said no to God. I cried, I prayed, I even yelled at God, but just as in the story of the call of Moses, God persisted: God's voice was strong even in the midst of chaos and my changing world.

We resist God's call in so many ways. We find every excuse in the book to put God off, including:

I am too old. Find someone younger! I know an elderly nun who lives in a convent in Ontario. She is very limited in her ability to do anything physical so she spends her day in prayer for the other sisters and the people whose names they bring to her.

I am too busy with my family and my job. Find someone else who has more time! There are women and men who choose to participate in church events and activities and make these events an important part of their family time.

I have never done that before. Surely there is someone else with more experience! Thank God for people who have taken a risk, reading in church or teaching Sunday school for the first time and learning more from these experiences than they ever thought possible.

I can't sing a note!

I can't read in public!

I am too young!

The list is endless. Who am I that I should go? I challenge you to consider what it is that you can do to become a servant for your church and community. Let your creative juices flow. Listen to what God is calling you to do.

OPENING REFLECTIONS

*Who in your life has been the messenger of
good news of the gospel of Jesus Christ?*

*How has this person (how have these persons)
influenced your life?*

What characteristics do you wish to emulate?

What is God's call in your life?

How are you responding to this call?

Meditation on the Promise

SEVERAL years ago I presided at a wedding in Kingston, Ontario. During the dinner that followed, Susan and I sat across from a woman who as it turned out worked for a film-distribution company in Quebec. She was very excited about a new French film, *La marche de l'empereur*. She raved about the music, the cinematography, and the story. She insisted that we go see it.

A few weeks later we were invited to share a meal with a group of friends. During the conversation they shared with us their excitement about having just seen *March of the Penguins*, the English version of the film.

Twice in a few weeks this unheard of movie was the centre of conversation! Needless to say, we went to see it.

The setting of the movie is the harsh, beautiful, unforgiving continent of Antarctica, where the winter temperatures can drop to minus eighty degrees Celsius, not counting wind chill. The skies remain dark for twenty-four hours a day for months, and very little life survives.

The story is about the amazing life cycle of emperor penguins. The cameras show the males marching across seventy miles of ice and snow to meet with the females at the breeding grounds, a place with ice thick enough to support the community. The mating season is short before the onslaught of severe winter with its cold wind and total darkness. After months of gestation, the single egg is "born" and is passed from the female to the male for care. The females then leave for the seventy-mile trek back to open water to find food.

Meanwhile, for the entire time that the females are away, the males must balance the egg on top of their feet (to keep it from touching the ground and freezing) and beneath their torso (to keep it warm). They do this for several months until the females return, to feed the newly born penguins. If the males or the young penguins could talk, surely they would shout as they watched the females returning after the months of waiting, "How beautiful are the feet of those who bring good food!" When the females return with food for the new babes, it is not a minute too soon. Their very survival depends on it. It is now the mothers' turn to stay and care for the young, as the fathers, now weak and starving, begin the long trek to the feeding grounds some seventy miles away.

The Apostle Paul says to the church in Rome, "How beautiful are the feet of those who bring good news!" (Rom. 10:15) He had been converted from a strict belief in Judaism in his historic "road to Damascus experience." After that time he devoted his life to walking,

> *"How beautiful are the feet of those who bring good news."*

sailing, travelling, preaching, and writing letters, all in the single cause of **bringing the good news** of the birth and life and resurrection of Jesus, the Messiah.

The word *Messiah* comes from a Greek transliteration, μεσσιασ, of a Hebrew word, *hammasiah*, denoting an anointed person. The Hebrew word is usually translated in Greek as Χριστοσ, the Christ. Therefore the name Jesus Christ literally means Jesus, the Messiah, the anointed one.

Scripture tells us that God anointed Jesus of Nazareth with the Holy Spirit and with power. It tells us how Jesus "went about doing good and healing all who were oppressed by the devil, for God was with him" (Acts 10:38). Jesus himself reminded his listeners as he began his public ministry that God had anointed him. Quoting from Isaiah, he says (Lk. 4:18):

> The Spirit of the Lord is upon me, because he has anointed me to bring good news to the poor. He has sent me to proclaim release to the captives and recovery of sight to the blind, to let the oppressed go free ...

The act of anointing is not new. Many centuries before Jesus, "Moses ordained and anointed Aaron with holy oil; it was an everlasting covenant for him and for his descendants as long as the heavens endure, to minister to the Lord and serve as priest and bless his people in his name" (Sirach 45:15).

104 We, the members of the body of Christ, the church, εκκλεσια, the ecclesia, continue to be baptized and anointed as God's chosen, just as Christians have been for centuries.[76] As parents and teachers, we too assume the mantle of sharing and caring for those God has entrusted to us. Children are held above the cold and hurt by caring parents; they are fed and nurtured, first with physical and then with spiritual food; they are embraced and upheld

---

76 2 Cor. 1:21: "But it is God who establishes us with you in Christ and has anointed us ..."

not just by loving parents and caregivers, but, like emperor penguins, by supportive and caring communities. This is how our children grow and learn.

The devotion and dedication that the biological parents show the baby penguins is astonishing, but no less so is the sense of community involvement in mutually nurturing and protecting this new life. And so it is with us. We are born into our respective families and wider communities not by choice but by grace. Our physical and spiritual well being depend on a supportive and nurturing intimate environment and a broader community that is bound by the innate, inherent, and timeless values of love and care.

This is the community, the *ecclesia* (εκκλησια), which all baptized Christians enter. We become heirs to the promise of the Anointed One, the Christ, who said, "... Let the little children come to me" (Mk. 10:14).

*How beautiful are the feet of those who feed
the hungry*

*How beautiful are the feet of those who
nurture the children*

*How beautiful are the feet of those who teach
in his name, and who clothe the naked*

*How beautiful are the feet of those who speak
in the name of justice and free the oppressed.*

Let us give thanks for family and community who have nourished and supported us. Let us remember the promise of salvation as promised by our Lord, the Anointed One, the risen Saviour, and the Prince of Peace.

CLOSING REFLECTIONS

Irma is a member of a Canadian Pentecostal church. As her church grew, the board decided to undertake a major capital improvement program to accommodate church growth. As a part of this rejuvenation project, the church wanted to provide a place for people to gather outside of worship and study time. The plan called for the establishment of a coffee shop with a spacious seating area and full audio-visual facilities.

Irma was asked if she would volunteer as the leader / co-coordinator of the new operation, and after much prayer and discernment, Irma accepted the position. After several years, Irma's ministry of hospitality has touched hundreds. Not only does she organize and manage the refreshment centre, she also takes time to mentor and witness to young and old alike. Her life inside and outside the church is a true testimony to her faith and to God's promise that the good news will be proclaimed. She has been truly recognized as one who brings good news. It had been a lifelong dream of hers to run a coffee shop. She never dreamed it would be as a volunteer in a church setting. How beautiful are the feet that bring good news!

Can you relate to Irma's story? How have you responded when opportunities for service have presented themselves in your church, community, or home?

The Bible tells us that we must share the good news of the Lord, so that people might know him (Rom. 10:14). How do you personally share the good news of salvation made known through belief in Christ? (Rom. 10:13)

How has your church community shared the good news of salvation made known through belief in Christ? (Rom. 10:13)

Write about people you know who have blessed communities of faith through mutual care and nurture.

What are the qualities about these persons that you admire or hope to emulate?

9

A CALL TO WORSHIP, HOLINESS, AND UNITY

Romans 12:1-8

Romans 12:1-8

¹I appeal to you therefore, brothers and sisters, by the mercies of God, to present your bodies as a living sacrifice, holy and acceptable to God, which is your spiritual worship. ²Do not be conformed to this world, but be transformed by the renewing of your minds, so that you may discern what is the will of God – what is good and acceptable and perfect. ³For by the grace given to me I say to everyone among you not to think of yourself more highly than you ought to think, but to think with sober judgment, each according to the measure of faith that God has assigned. ⁴For as in one body we have many members, and not all the members have the same function, ⁵so we, who are many, are one body in Christ, and individually we are members one of another. ⁶We have gifts that differ according to the grace given to us: prophecy, in proportion to faith; ⁷ministry, in ministering; the teacher, in teaching; ⁸the exhorter, in exhortation; the giver, in generosity; the leader, in diligence; the compassionate, in cheerfulness.

GOD'S PROMISE

God promises that your "gifts" are truly valued in the church.

ROMANS 12:6

FOCUS

Paul's appeal to the church to discern the will of God.

THEOLOGICAL BACKGROUND

What does it mean to worship God? The ancient Greek word for worship, λατρεια, is very interesting. It meant "the state of a hired laborer, service." The Greek for worship of God meant "service to the gods, divine worship" (Plato, *Apologia*, 23 C).[77]

The Greek New Testament uses the same word but gives it the meaning "service or worship of God."[78]

The English word *worship* means "reverent honor and homage paid to God ..." The word is derived from the Middle English word *weorthscipe*: worth ship; worth, merit; ship, character.[79]

The following scripture references show the importance that our ancestors in faith placed on true worship of God:

> God tells Moses to say to Pharaoh, "The LORD, the God of the Hebrews, sent me to you to say, 'Let my people go, so that they may **worship** me in the wilderness.' " (Ex. 7:16)

---

77 Liddell et al. *A Greek-English Lexicon*, 1032.
78 Bauer et al., *A Greek-English Lexicon of the New Testament, and Other Early Christian Literature*, 467.
79 *Random House Unabridged Dictionary*, 2191.

Pharaoh's officials say to Pharaoh, "How long shall this fellow be a snare to us? Let the people go, so that they may **worship** the LORD their God; do you not yet understand that Egypt is ruined?" (Ex. 10:7)

The Psalmist says, "Extol the LORD our God; **worship** at his footstool. Holy is he!" (Ps. 99:5)

Jesus says to the devil, "Away with you, Satan! For it is written, '**worship** the Lord your God, and serve only him.' " (Mt. 4:10)

Jesus says to the Samaritan woman, "God is spirit, and those who **worship** him must **worship** in spirit and truth." (Jn. 4:24)

Paul says to the Romans, "I appeal to you therefore, brothers and sisters, by the mercies of God, to present your bodies as a living sacrifice, holy and acceptable to God, which is your spiritual **worship**." (Rom. 12:1)

Paul says to the Corinthians, "After the secrets of the unbeliever's heart are disclosed, that person will bow down before God and **worship** him, declaring, 'God is really among you.' " (1 Cor. 14:25)

Paul says to Timothy, "I am grateful to God – whom I **worship** with a clear conscience, as my ancestors did – when I remember you constantly in my prayers night and day." (2 Tim. 1:3)

One of the Elders tells John that those singing to God have come through "the great ordeal" and that, "For this reason they are before the throne of God, and **worship** him day and night within his temple, and the one who is seated on the throne will shelter them." (Rev. 7:15)

OPENING REFLECTIONS

How do you live out your Christian faith in these areas?

Generosity

Diligence

Cheerfulness

Patience

Faith

Paul speaks of "a measure of faith" being given to each believer (Rom. 12:3). What does it mean to have faith as a Christian? What does it mean for you?

Meditation on the Promise

IN this chapter's passage from Romans, Paul appeals to the church, "by the mercies of God ... to discern what is the will of God – what is good and acceptable and perfect" (Rom. 12:1-2). You might say to yourself, "This text is meant for someone else or for another church." I want to examine that assumption.

This powerful text could be summarized as God's call to **worship, holiness, and unity**. I want to begin by looking at examples from three distinct eras to show how these attributes are indeed applicable to all churches today.

WORSHIP: A CONTEMPORARY PERSPECTIVE

I have written elsewhere that the theologian Douglas John Hall's greatest criticism of liberal mainline denominations in North America is

> their attraction and nurture of well-meaning good-living people who worship by rote, who engage in lukewarm worship, and fail to connect in any real way with the *disturbing presence* of ministry demanded through following Christ's example ...[80]

114

---

80 McAllister, *Revival of Wexford Heights United Church*, 146. As Anthony J. Gittins writes in *A Presence That Disturbs*, "It might be argued that the Spirit is trying to break through and speak to us in all manner of people and situations but that humanity – and the institutional church – is blocking, or muzzling, the Spirit" (29). "It is important to reiterate that true Christian discipleship is not measured simply by the capacity to be a presence that disturbs others; we must first have felt God's disturbing presence within ourselves" (43).

Hall also writes about the response to the demise of Christendom by a faction he calls the "Back to Christendom" movement, who attribute the humiliation and decline of Christendom to

> the laxity and wishy-washiness of liberal and moderate forms of Christianity. Mainstream Protestantism is failing, they assert, because it has become so indistinct, so lacking in conviction, so much a part of the sociological wallpaper that its message consists of little more than stained-glass versions of ever-changing values and trends by which the greater society is continually titillated.[81]

HOLINESS: JOHN FLETCHER AND JOHN WESLEY

Going back to eighteenth-century England, consider two preachers and theologians who were instrumental in the reform of church and society. "Wesley and Fletcher wrote about, taught, preached, and led by example as they encouraged people to strive toward a life of holiness, enjoy the fruits of the Spirit, and to grow in faith as they sought salvation. They both believed in the power of the Holy Spirit, the centrality of the grace of God, and the foundational nature of Holy Scriptures."[82]

Has the church lost its sense of reverence for the sanctuary? Have we lost that idea of holiness in our churches or the idea of the potential for holiness within each person? "Wesley and Fletcher's concept of holiness means nothing to a society that believes in 'progress at all costs.' "[83]

---

81 Hall and Reuther, *God and the Nations*, 50.
82 McAllister, *Revival of Wexford Heights United Church*, 170.
83 *Ibid.*, 215.

Unity: Ancient Truths from the Apostle Paul

The Apostle Paul believed that the church must live as a single community. He believed that the Christian community must be shaped by the Messiah himself. Christians must strive for unity, "which must come through the humility in which each thinks soberly about his or her own gifts and role, rather than placing too high a value on them."[84] "To be "in Christ," as here, is to be a member of the Messiah's people, to speak of "one body in Christ" is to emphasize the unity of that people despite its obvious diversity.[85] For Paul, unity in the church is attained through people exercising their gifts.[86]

What has your church's experience been with respect to **worship, holiness, and unity**? Let us explore this chapter's text, Romans 12:1-8, in more detail. The opening verse indicates that the foundation of all Christian obedience, "that those in Christ, indwelt by the Spirit, are to offer to God the true sacrificial worship."[87] Paul is very blunt in his directions to the church, "What a Christian does, in Christ and by the Spirit, gives actual pleasure to God."[88] That is why it is important for us as Christians and as a Christian community that we pay attention to Paul's advice in these matters of worship, holiness, and unity. This is difficult because we are conditioned and influenced by the forces of the world, which Paul refers to as the spirit of the flesh. We bring these behaviours and experiences into our Christian communities. This is why Paul encourages us to be *transformed*.

---

84 *The New Interpreter's Bible*, X, 708.
85 *Ibid.*, 710.
86 *Ibid.*, 702.
87 *Ibid.*, 704.
88 *Ibid.*

The first verse describes our bodies as being "holy and acceptable to God," this being our "spiritual act of worship." The second verse talks about our transformation by the renewing of the mind. "Reasonable worship focuses on the **renewal of the mind**, but the result is that people being thus **transformed**, can work out in practice what is the right thing to do."[89] This means that if the body of Christ is not acting in a right manner, then the body and mind of the people are not transformed, and thus there is much to be undertaken as the body of Christ with respect to **worship, holiness, and unity**.

Paul shifts the focus from pleasing ourselves to pleasing God. "What proceeds from the transformed mind does indeed reflect the image of God."[90] Paul also writes about a measure of faith. What does it mean to have faith as a Christian? What does it mean for you? Paul answers this question in the early part of Romans (3:27-28):

> Then what becomes of boasting? It is excluded. By what law? By what works? No, but by the law of faith. For we hold that a person is justified by faith apart from works prescribed by the law.

But what is faith? Paul answers this by stating that faith is the same for everybody: "Believe that Jesus is Lord and that God raised him from the dead."[91] Having this faith does not set you apart from other believers. For Paul each member is a part of the body, and each member has gifts that are of value to the community. Paul lists seven gifts: prophecy, ministry, teaching, exhortation, giving, leading,

---

89 *Ibid.*, 705.
90 *Ibid.*
91 Rom. 10:9-10: "Because if you confess with your lips that Jesus is Lord and believe in your heart that God raised him from the dead, you will be saved. For one believes with the heart and so is justified, and one confesses with the mouth and so is saved."

and compassion, indicating the completeness of God's provision for the work of the church.[92] How do we exercise our gifts within the community of faith? We may try to fool our neighbours or ourselves, but God knows our true hearts. (See chapter 3 above, "Where Is Your Heart?")

Paul says givers should be generous, leaders should be diligent, and compassion should be shown cheerfully. For Paul the Christian life is not simply a pursuit of individual virtue but a concern with building up the community as a whole. How can we not feel overwhelmed by the density and power of Romans and the seeming impossibility of being the Christians Paul charges us to be? Where can we start, knowing that, as Paul says in Romans 3:23, we "all have sinned and fall short of the glory of God"? The answer is found in Paul's simple yet powerful statement in Romans 12:5: "Individually we are members one of another." Paul also gives us guidelines to help us shape our character and response as we live our life: to be generous, diligent, cheerful, patient, and faithful.

Be generous in spirit and truth: What does it mean to be generous as a Christian? It means to think of the needs of others and to do our best to help others through gifts of time, energy, and money. These acts of kindness come with practice. You have heard it said that the Lord loves a cheerful giver. What good are your gifts of service if they come from a grumpy spirit?

Be diligent: To be diligent is to be industrious, thorough, attentive, and careful. The opposite is to be lazy. A diligent

---

92 *The New Interpreter's Bible*, X, 710. As a note of interest, this list is different from gifts listed in Paul's other letters. It is important to note that "just as God has given him [Paul] grace for his task, so God gives the church grace for its multiple and mutually supportive tasks, and whatever they are they must be exercised to the full extent of one's powers."

Christian will be disciplined about Bible study, prayer, church attendance, and spending time with God. These are all spiritual disciplines that lead us in the paths of righteousness and toward a life of holiness.

Be cheerful: Being cheerful is healthful and life giving. You know how you feel when you enter into a place where people are happy – where they genuinely love what they are doing.

I remember a cartoon I saw with an elderly minister in the pulpit, drawn and haggard with a day-old beard saying to his congregation with a sad demeanour, "Make a joyful noise unto the Lord." We often fail to worship and praise our God with true joy in our hearts. What a blessing it is to enter the house of the Lord and find the joy-filled spirit of worship. I love the song, "I've got the joy, joy, joy, joy, down in my heart!"

Be patient: Paul speaks about the need for patience (Rom. 8:25). This is a difficult one for many of us. We live in an

Instant coffee

Much music

Drive-thru

Express lane

Quick Mart kind of world.

A yellow light means step on the pedal and drive faster

Long line-ups mean high blood pressure and

Long weekends mean stop-and-go traffic.

We become very impatient when things do not move as fast as we want. Think about how you feel when you are waiting in a supermarket checkout.

Stephen A. McAllister

Stopping to look watch the sun set

Listening to the plaintive sound of the
white-throated sparrow

Catching a glimpse of a child's smile

Hearing God's whisper speak through the
silence of scripture

Holding the hand of an elderly patient, and
Praying, listening, waiting, and learning
– all of these take patience.

120

Be faithful: "Do not think of yourself more highly than you ought to think, but ... with sober judgment, each according to the measure of faith that God has assigned" (Rom. 12:3). Remember, faith is the same for everybody, for all are to believe that Jesus is Lord and that God raised him from the dead. You cannot prove this; it calls for faith through belief.

I said earlier that you may think that this text is meant for someone else, or another church. Do you have any room to improve your Christian living in these areas?

Generosity

Diligence

Cheerfulness

Patience

Faith.

These are important aspects of the Christian life. Paul says in Romans 10:10 that justification comes from believing "with the heart" and salvation comes from confessing "with the mouth."

This is the good news of the gospel – the good news for you today. This is the news that will bring you encouragement as you worship with sincerity, as your church community grows in holiness through God's invitation to communion, repentance, and pardon.

Deepening communion

Growth in love of God and neighbour, and

Growth in unity, the unity of Christ.

This is the free gift of God to you this day: worship, holiness, and unity.

CLOSING REFLECTIONS

Carla and Phillip are lay leaders in their rural Presbyterian church in eastern Canada. In the last few years they decided that they needed to become more involved as a married couple in the life and work of their church. When approached by their minister to see if they would be willing to assist in leadership roles, they both said yes. Carla and

Phillip work tirelessly to support the ministry and enable leaders and empower volunteers. They lead by example as they respond to the church's call to worship, holiness, and unity. They truly understand God's promise that people's gifts are valued in the church, and through their witness and example they bless many lives.

Burnout is a big problem for most churches. Think about how the leaders in your church manage the affairs of the church and how they reflect the ideals that Paul identified in the areas of worship, holiness, and unity.

Reflect on the following statement. Does it apply to your church community / denomination?

My congregation / denomination attracts and nurtures well-meaning good-living people who worship by rote, who engage in lukewarm worship, and fail to connect in any real way with the disturbing presence of ministry demanded through following Christ's example.

Reflect on the following:

I believe in the power of the Holy Spirit.
I believe in the centrality of the grace of God.
I believe in the foundational nature of the Holy
  Scriptures.

How can you improve your Christian living
in the areas of:

Generosity

Diligence

Cheerfulness

Patience

Faith

What is the biggest challenge/opportunity for your church in the areas of:

Worship

Holiness

Unity

10

MISSION IMPOSSIBLE

Romans 12:9-21

Romans 12:9-21

⁹Let love be genuine; hate what is evil, hold fast to what is good; ¹⁰love one another with mutual affection; outdo one another in showing honor. ¹¹Do not lag in zeal, be ardent in spirit, serve the Lord. ¹²Rejoice in hope, be patient in suffering, persevere in prayer. ¹³Contribute to the needs of the saints; extend hospitality to strangers. ¹⁴Bless those who persecute you; bless and do not curse them. ¹⁵Rejoice with those who rejoice, weep with those who weep. ¹⁶Live in harmony with one another; do not be haughty, but associate with the lowly; do not claim to be wiser than you are. ¹⁷Do not repay anyone evil for evil, but take thought for what is noble in the sight of all. ¹⁸If it is possible, so far as it depends on you, live peaceably with all. ¹⁹Beloved, never avenge yourselves, but leave room for the wrath of God; for it is written, "Vengeance is mine, I will repay, says the Lord." ²⁰No, "if your enemies are hungry, feed them; if they are thirsty, give them something to drink; for by doing this you will heap burning coals on their heads." ²¹Do not be overcome by evil, but overcome evil with good.

GOD'S PROMISE

Love will overcome evil.

ROMANS 12:21

FOCUS

Paul's final word of encouragement: "Do not be overcome by evil, but overcome evil with good."

THEOLOGICAL BACKGROUND

God speaks about overcoming evil with love. What is evil? We read this about it in the book of Genesis (3:22):

Then the LORD God said, "See, the man has become like one of us, knowing good and evil ..."

As a result, God "drove out the man" (Gen. 3:24). The word *evil* is found 613 times in the King James Version of the Bible. The word *love* is found 310 times in that version.The Greek word for *evil* is κακοσ, and it has many meanings:

bad, worthless, corrupt, depraved (Mt. 21:41; 24:48; Mk. 7:21)

wicked, criminal, morally bad; evil, wickedness, crime (Mt. 27:23; Acts 23:9)

deceitful (1 Pet. 3:10)

mischievous; harmful, destructive; mischief, harm, injury (Titus 1:12)

evil, misery, affliction, suffering (Lk. 16:25).[93]

127

93 Mounce, *The Analytical Lexicon to the Greek New Testatment*, 261.

We pray, "Deliver us from the evil one" when we say the Lord's Prayer.[94] The church believes passionately in the forgiveness of sins. The Bible says sin and the effects of sin are pervasive in the life of the righteous. To be righteous is not a matter of being sinless but a matter of humbly and honestly confessing our transgressions to the Lord and receiving God's forgiveness (Ps. 32).[95] Jesus himself blessed the disciples and directed them to engage in the ministry of forgiveness:

> Jesus said to them again, "Peace be with you. As the Father has sent me, so I send you." When he had said this, he breathed on them and said to them, "Receive the Holy Spirit. If you forgive the sins of any, they are forgiven them; if you retain the sins of any, they are retained." (Jn. 20:21-23)

OPENING REFLECTIONS

How do the rules and regulations of the church exclude the very people Jesus served with so much passion and love?

---

94 Matt. 6:13: "And do not bring us to the time of trial, but rescue us from the evil one." του πονηρου: Greek words for "the evil one." *The Greek New Testament*, 18
95 *The New Interpreter's Bible*, IV, 805.

Why is it so difficult to live in harmony with our neighbours? Think of:

Communities (consider the neighbourhood violence we hear reported each evening on the news)

Homes (consider the amount of domestic violence) and

Churches (beginning with Paul's reports of factions and divisions in the church).

Reflect on Jesus' direction to the disciples to engage in a ministry of forgiveness. Is it difficult to either (a) forgive or (b) accept forgiveness? If so, why?

Meditation on the Promise

Several years ago, I moved to Chicago to begin doctoral studies in ministry at Catholic Theological Union, the largest Roman Catholic graduate school of theology and ministry in North America. My experience was rich as I studied and communed with colleagues from many countries of the world, including Nigeria, Zambia, Vietnam, China, Indonesia, Philippines, India, and the United States. In some ways this new venture in the Lord's service felt like mission impossible.

Mission Impossible, a seven-year TV series that began in 1966, chronicled the adventures of the Impossible Missions Force (IMF), a team of government spies and specialists who were assigned missions by the unseen Secretary. I especially remember Peter Graves in his role as Jim Phelps, team leader.

The Mission Impossible team

The series is best known for its opening mission assignment (conducted by tape recording), the leader's selection of mission agents from a dossier, the opening briefing, and the intricate use of disguises. I can vividly remember the excitement I felt as the music played while the final instructions were being read from the tape recorder:

> Your mission, Jim, should you decide to accept it, is ... Should you or any member of your I.M. Force be caught or killed, the Secretary will disavow any knowledge of your actions. This tape will self-destruct in five seconds. Good luck, Jim.

Paul the Apostle's instructions to the church did not self-destruct in five seconds; to the contrary, his letters to the early Christian communities have survived for almost two thousand years. Today God continues to use Paul – this convert to Christianity, this complex and direct-speaking individual – to teach and inform Christian communities around the world.

Indeed, the text of this final chapter is dense with meaning, with much to say to Christian communities today. In fact, this text is about *community*. The focus is on *genuine love*, which is the only appropriate response to the gift of God in Christ. This part of his letter contains counsel to the church in Rome, a church that was probably struggling with how to accommodate both Jews and Greeks. Paul writes to the church in Rome with news of "God's power of salvation to the Jew first and also to the Greek" (Rom. 1:16). Paul had experienced conflict and tension in other church communities. He brackets this part of his letter with these admonitions to the Roman community: "Let love be genuine; hate what is evil" (Rom. 12:9) and "Do not be overcome by evil, but overcome evil with good" (Rom. 12:21). Therein lies the mission impossible for humanity: to overcome evil with good!

We see examples of this daily in the lives of nations, families, and people as they try to solve problems through conflict and violence. In recent years, there have been conflict and strife in Iraq, Darfur, Pakistan, the Middle East, and Sri Lanka, to name just a few. In the city of Toronto, gang / turf violence continues to claim the lives of young people and innocent bystanders. The daily news reminds us that there is always a war going on somewhere in the world. One subsides, another breaks out. Often lost in the sheer magnitude of global violence is its devastating and increasing impact on children. An estimated two million children have died in the last decade and 250,000 have been forced to participate in fighting.[96]

There are dark forces at work in this world and, sadly, we can look within ourselves and find sin. Paul speaks of sinister forces that creep into the church and the conflict and evil that may lurk within church communities. (Read Dietrich Bonhoeffer's commentary on this in the Opening Reflection of chapter 6.)

The Bible is not afraid to talk about evil. Evil, in all of its forms and ramifications is a real part of life. Evil is a force that must be fought in every way and in every place. Paul saw the church, the body of Christ, as the place where the forces of good could coalesce and be mustered, rallied, and focused in this spiritual battle. "Put on the whole armor of God," he writes in Ephesians 6:11, "so that you may be able to stand against the wiles of the devil."

I want to focus in this chapter on Paul's teaching about community. For Paul, love, not fake love, not mushy love, not sexual love, not selfish love, but *genuine love*, plays out in relationships within community, the community of faith known as the τη εκκλησια, the ecclesia, the place where:

---

96 Sutton-Redner, "Children in a World of Violence."

*People go out of their way to show deep respect
to the one another.*

Love is active, seeking out opportunities to serve.

*Love contributes to the needs of the saints (a term
Paul used to describe members of the Christian
communities in Rome, Corinth, Ephesus, Philippi,
and Colossae).*

And people:
> *are "aglow in the Spirit"*
> *outdo one another in showing respect*
> *look for ways to show hospitality*
> *seek to serve the lowly, and*

*are faithful in prayer, led by love, and supported
in hope, making them steadfast in adversity.*

The purpose of love, for Paul, is not selfish; it is to promote the welfare of our neighbours and to build up the congregation.[97] The implication is that anything we do to disrupt the fellowship and distress the community and its ministry is contrary to God's will. The will of God is for the church to be a fellowship of peace, and for the fellowship to build each other up in love. This must be done in an attitude of mutual respect and harmony. This is God's plan for us and for all peoples of the earth.

I experienced this respect and harmony at Catholic Theological Union. Priests, ministers, and lay people gathered from around the world to worship and pray together; we were open to learning about the kingdom of God in our midst. A powerful moment occurred early one morning during worship as the words from Ecclesiastes were read: "For everything there is a season, and a time for every matter under heaven ..." (Eccl. 3:1). You probably

133

---
97 Bryan, *A Preface to Romans*, 197.

know the words a few verses later, in 3:5: "a time to throw away stones, and a time to gather stones together ..." When this sentence was read, I had this vision of people all over the world dropping their stones, their guns, and their swords, and walking back to the table where they might enjoy a meal together to just "be together."

Jesus was wise when he gathered the faithful around a table, as we often do in community and the church, to share a meal in remembrance of the one who came to bring peace. I sat between two priests at dinner that weekend, one from Zambia and one from India, two countries I have never visited, and marvelled at both our differences and our similarities.[98]

I want to look at two major points in Paul's letter that are extremely difficult for us. The first is Paul's warning to individuals within the community to not become wise in their own thoughts. He writes, "Live in harmony with one another; do not be haughty, but associate with the lowly; do not claim to be wiser than you are" (Rom. 12:16). Here Paul is referring to words from the book of Proverbs: "Do not be wise in your own eyes; fear the LORD, and turn away from evil" (Prov. 3:7).

Leon Morris writes in his commentary on Romans about the problem that occurs in church communities when people become "wise in their own eyes."[99] This is something that inevitably makes people resistant to perceiving and accepting God's plans, which consistently confound and overthrow human wisdom. This is a stumbling block in many Christian communities, where the community leaders have become wise in their own thoughts and thus become resistant to God's word and will.

---

98 Sadly, the Indian priest was recently killed in a tragic pedestrian / car accident while serving in missionary work in the United States.

99 Morris, *The Epistle to the Romans*, 44.

This is a very difficult frame of mind to resist, because we are taught from a young age to be deliberate, intentional, and to work with reason and purpose. This leads people in organizations to become self-confident and single-minded, to the point where the organization begins to take on the personality of the leaders. Christian communities suffer in a controlled environment, yet the church cannot stifle the Holy Spirit! Paul knows the will of God as taught in the scriptures. He understands that we must remain open to God's teachings and that this is possible only when we are in a spirit of openness and humility. This truth is unchangeable and cannot be denied!

The second critical point for Paul is that people should not repay evil for evil. Paul drops the bombshell in verse 17: "Do not repay anyone evil for evil, but take thought for what is noble in the sight of all." This leads us into a truly difficult area of thought. This is virtually mission impossible – hence the continued chaos in our world, our cities, our homes, and our places of worship. People find it virtually impossible to do what Jesus himself modelled. Jesus himself, even unto death, forgave those who persecuted him. While dying on the cross he said, "Father, forgive them; for they know not what they are doing" (Lk. 23:34).

As Morris notes,

> to be overcome by evil means to respond to evil with evil, and evil simply increases. To retaliate when someone hurts, is to be overcome, not to win, because it brings one down to the level of the other.[100]

Mahatma Gandhi was one of the last century's greatest proponents of non-violence. He is quoted as saying:

---
100 *Ibid.*

"Victory attained by violence is tantamount to a defeat, for it is momentary."[101]

Mahatma Gandhi

Even though we are urged by Paul to live in peace, "peace at the price of the sacrifice of truth or the compromise of principle is not asked for."[102] I suppose this is why Jesus challenged and pushed people in many settings to put the welfare and sanctity of people, especially the marginalized, ahead of structures and rules. Jesus fought against the powers and principalities in the world, which sought "power over" rather than "power with."[103]

New power, says Paul, comes from the love that the Holy Spirit brings. The way to overcome evil is with love. The way of love lifts us above all vindictiveness and thus frees us, soul and body, to live in peace and focus on the good and the mission of Christ. This is mission impossible.

As we enter this new day, let us give thanks to the Apostle Paul for his deep words of wisdom. To paraphrase Jim Phelps in a prayerful manner:

---

101 Gandhi, *The Collected Works of Mahatma Gandhi.*
102 *Ibid.*
103 For an excellent study on the subject of mutuality dealing with issues of power, see Nothwehr, *Mutuality.*

Your mission, people of God, should you decide to accept it, is to:

> *love one another with mutual affection*
>
> *outdo one another in showing honour*
>
> *be ardent in spirit; serve the Lord*
>
> *rejoice in hope*
>
> *be patient in suffering*
>
> *persevere in prayer*
>
> *contribute to the needs of the saints*
>
> *extend hospitality to strangers*
>
> *bless those who persecute you; bless and do not curse them*
>
> *live in harmony with one another*
>
> *avoid:*
>
> > *being haughty, but associate with the lowly claiming to be wiser than you are*
> >
> > *repaying anyone evil for evil.*

Take thought for what is noble in the sight of all.

137

As usual, should you or any member of your community feel discouraged, Jesus Christ our Lord will be with you until the end of the age. The Spirit of the Lord is upon you.

Amen.

Closing Reflections

Norman is a chaplain in a regional correctional facility in the American midwest. He works tirelessly as he counsels, listens, encourages, and mentors the men and women inmates, many of whom have known and seen great evil in their lives. Many of them have heard the good news of God's love made known through Jesus Christ and have made a formal commitment to turn from sin and darkness and embrace a new life. Norman's life witness to inmates, families, visitors, colleagues, and staff reminds us of God's promise that the way to overcome evil is with love.

This chaplain works in an environment where few people minister. How is his job like Mission Impossible? How does he do it?

This chapter speaks about the vision of people dropping their stones and joining together in peace and harmony around a communal meal. Could you invite Norman's released "congregation" to your church's communal meal and truly embrace these men and women?

What stones are you carrying that you would like to drop?

Who in your life would you like to bring back into your communal place of fellowship or community?

What is the mission impossible in your:

Spiritual life

Church life

Personal life

When and how do you actually engage with the marginalized?

The Apostle Paul writes about our propensity to "become wise in our own eyes" and names this as a stumbling block to Christian living. Why is this so? What does this mean to you?

Concluding Reflections

1. What are your key learnings from this study?

2. What you have learned about the Epistle to the Romans?

3. How has your understanding of Paul's wisdom for the church and / or your life changed?

4. What questions you would like to ask the Apostle Paul?

5. *How has your understanding changed about what it means to be a Christian?*

6. *In what ways has your faith changed over the course of the study?*

7. *Write about your new understanding of God's promises for you.*

8. *What changes would you suggest for this study? Please send suggestions and comments to Stephen at srministries@gmail.com*

APPENDIX
WHAT *HAS* GOD PROMISED?

WHEN I lead a group using this book I am asked many questions about the history of Paul's letter to the church in Rome. Why did Paul write the book? What is his underlying theology? (This takes us into the subjects covered in the theological background sections of each chapter in this book.) People also ask the broader question, what does God promise in the Bible as a whole?

To answer *that* question I refer people to the many places where the biblical writers speak of God and his direct promises. I group these verses into themes, noting that God promises land and inheritance, blessing, hope, the Word, and finally Jesus and the Holy Spirit.

LAND AND INHERITANCE

Deuteronomy 6:3: Hear therefore, O Israel, and observe [God's decrees and commandments] diligently, so that it may go well with you, and so that you may multiply greatly in a land flowing with milk and honey, as the LORD, the **God** of your ancestors, has **promised** you.

Deuteronomy 9:5: It is not because of your righteousness or the uprightness of your heart that you are going in to occupy their land; but because of the wickedness of these nations the LORD your **God** is dispossessing them before you, in order to fulfill the **promise** that the LORD made on oath to your ancestors, to Abraham, to Isaac, and to Jacob.

Deuteronony 12:20: When the LORD your **God** enlarges your territory, as he has **promised** you ...

Joshua 23:5: ... and you shall possess their land, as the LORD your **God promised** you.

Galatians 3:18: For if the inheritance comes from the law, it no longer comes from the **promise**; but **God** granted it to Abraham through the **promise**.

Hebrews 6:13-14: When **God** made a **promise** to Abraham, because he had no one greater by whom to swear, he swore by himself, saying, "I will surely bless you and multiply you."

BLESSING

Genesis 12:1: Now the LORD said to Abram, "Go from your country and your kindred and your father's house to the land that I will show you. I will make of you a great nation, and I will **bless** you, and make your name great, so that you will be a **blessing**.

Deuteronomy 1:11: May the LORD, the **God** of your ancestors, increase you a thousand times more and bless you, as he has **promised** you!

Deuteronomy 15:6: When the LORD your **God** has **blessed** you, as he **promised you** ...

Deuteronomy 19:8: If the LORD your **God** enlarges your territory, as he swore to your ancestors – and he will give you all the land that he **promised** your ancestors to give you ...

1 Chronicles 17:26: And now, O LORD, you are **God**, and you have **promised** this good thing to your servant ...

HOPE

Acts 26:6: And now I stand here on trial on account of my hope in the **promise** made by **God** to our ancestors ...

Ephesians 2:12: ... remember that you were at that time without Christ, being aliens from the commonwealth of Israel, and strangers to the covenants of **promise**, having no hope and without **God** in the world.

THE WORD

1 Kings 8:26: Therefore, O **God** of Israel, let your word be confirmed, which you **promised** to your servant my father David.

JESUS

Acts 13:23: Of this man's posterity **God** has brought to Israel a Savior, Jesus, as he **promised** ...

THE HOLY SPIRIT

Acts 2:33: Being therefore exalted at the right hand of **God**, and having received from the Father the **promise** of the Holy Spirit, he has poured out this that you both see and hear.

BIBLIOGRAPHY

The Anchor Bible Dictionary (New York: Doubleday, 1992).

Cassell's German-English, English-German Dictionary, Harold T. Betteridge, ed. (New York: Macmillan, 1978).

The Greek New Testament, Kurt Aland and Universität Münster, Institut für Neutestamentliche Textforschung (New York: United Bible Societies, 1983).

The New Interpreter's Bible: A Commentary in Twelve Volumes (Nashville: Abingdon, 2002).

The New Oxford Annotated Bible with the Apocryphal / Deuterocanonical Books, Michael David Coogan et al. (New York: Oxford University Press, 2001).

Random House Unabridged Dictionary, Stuart Berg Flexner and Leonore Crary Hauck, eds. (New York: Random House, 1993).

The Tanakh: A New Translation of the Holy Scriptures According to the Traditionial Hebrew Text (Philadelphia: Jewish Publication Society, 1985).

The Torah: A Modern Commentary, Plant, W. Gunter et al., eds. (New York: Union of American Hebrew Congregations, 1981).

Abraham, William J. and Hill, Ron, *Wesley for Armchair Theologians* (Louisville: Westminster John Knox, 2005).

Bauer, Walter, Arndt, William, Ginegrich, F. Wilbur, *A Greek-English Lexicon of the New Testament, and Other Early Christian Literature* (Chicago: University of Chicago Press, 1957).

Berton, Pierre, *The Comfortable Pew: A Critical Look at Christianity and the Religious Establishment in the New Age* (Philadelphia: Lippincott, 1965).

Bethge, Eberhard and Barnett, Victoria, *Dietrich Bonhoeffer: Theologian, Christian, Man for His Times – A Biography* (Minneapolis: Fortress, 2000).

Bonhoeffer, Dietrich, *The Cost of Discipleship* (New York: Touchstone, 1995).

Bonhoeffer, Dietrich, *Letters and Papers from Prison, Enlarged Edition* (New York: Macmillan, 1971).

Browne, Francis, Engl. transl. of chorale text, *Jesu, meine Freude*, 2008, http://www.bach-cantatas.com/Texts/Chorale062-Eng3.htm

Bryan, Christopher, *A Preface to Romans: Notes on the Epistle in Its Literary and Cultural Setting* (New York: Oxford University Press, 2000).

Coffey, David, *Did You Receive the Holy Spirit When You Believed? Some Basic Questions for Pneumatology* (Milwaukee: Marquette University Press, 2005).

Collins, Kenneth J., *A Real Christian: The Life of John Wesley* (Nashville: Abingdon, 1999).

Congar, Yves, *I Believe in the Holy Spirit*, David Smith, transl. (New York: Crossroad, 1997).

Creal, Michael, *"The Comfortable Pew* Revisited," *Catholic New Times*, January 16, 2005, http://www. findarticles.com/p/articles/mi_m0MKY/is_1_29/ ai_n8706902

Dunn, James D.G., *The Theology of Paul the Apostle* (Grand Rapids: Eerdmans, 1998).

ekkleisa.co.uk, "Southern Baptists and Catholics Join US Church Decline Trend," 2009, http://www.ekklesia. co.uk/node/8828

Forbes, James, *The Holy Spirit and Preaching* (Nashville: Abingdon, 1989).

Gandhi, Mahatma, *The Collected Works of Mahatma Gandhi* (Satyagraha Leaflets), 1919, www.gandhiserve. org/cwmg/VOL018.PDF

Gittins, Anthony J., *A Presence That Disturbs* (Liguori: Liguroi/Triumph, 2002).

Hafner, Katie, "Texting May Be Taking a Toll," *New York Times*, May 25, 2009.

Hall, Douglas John, *Bound and Free: A Theologian's Journey* (Minneapolis: Fortress, 2005).

Hall, Douglas John, *Why Christian? For Those on the Edge of Faith* (Minneapolis: Fortress, 1998).

Hall, Douglas John, and Reuther, Rosemary Radford, *God and the Nations* (Minneapolis: Fortress, 1995).

Jones, G. Curtis and Jones, Paul H., *500 Illustrations: Stories from Life for Preaching and Teaching* (Nashville: Abingdon, 1998).

Liddell, Henry George et al., *A Greek-English Lexicon* (New York: Clarendon Press; Oxford University Press, 1996).

Lucado, Max, *In the Eye of the Storm: A Day in the Life of Jesus* (Dallas: Word, 1991).

lifesitenews.com, " 'Christianity in Europe Coming to an End': Vienna Cardinal," http://www.lifesitenews.com/Idn/2009/apr/09041410.html

Luther, Martin, *Commentary on the Epistle to the Romans* (Grand Rapids: Zondervan, 1954).

Luther, Martin, Preface to the Letter of St. Paul to the Romans, Brother Andrew Thornton, transl., http://www.ccel.org/l/luther/romans/pref_romans.html

Maddix, Thomas D., *Journey to Wholeness: Healing Body, Mind and Soul* (Ottawa: Novalis, 2003).

Marshall, Traute Maass, "Johann Franck (Hymn-Writer)," http://www.bach-cantatas.com/Lib/Franck-Johann.htm

McAllister, Stephen Arthur, *Revival of Wexford Heights United Church: Which Path Should It Take?*, Doctor of Ministry thesis (Chicago: Catholic Theological Union, 2007).

McManners, John, *The Oxford Illustrated History of Christianity* (New York: Oxford University Press, 1990).

Moltmann, Jürgen, *The Crucified God: The Cross of Christ as the Foundation and Criticism of Christian Theology* (Minneapolis: Fortress, 1993).

Morris, Leon, *The Epistle to the Romans* (Grand Rapids: Eerdmans, 1988).

Mounce, William D., *The Analytical Lexicon to the Greek New Testament* (Grand Rapids: Zondervan, 1993).

Nothwehr, Dawn M., *Mutuality: A Formal Norm for Christian Social Ethics* (San Francisco: Catholic Scholars Press, 1998).

Oren, Aryeh, "Johann Crüger (Hymn-Writer, Composer)," http://www.bach-cantatas.com/Lib/Cruger-Johann.htm

Rad, Gerhard von, *Genesis: A Commentary* (Philadelphia: Westminster, 1972).

scribd.com, "Steadfast Faithfulness," 2008, http://www.scribd.com/doc/7215751/Steadfast-Faithfulness

Sermonillustrations.com, "Complacency," http://www.sermonillustrations.com/a-z/c/complacency.htm

Sutton-Redner, Jane, *Children in a World of Violence* (Children in Need Inc., 2008), http://www.childreninneed.com/magazine/violence.html

Wesley, John, *The Journal of the Rev. John Wesley, A.M.* Vols. I-IV, (London: Dent, 1906 [1922]).

White, Hilary, " 'Christianity in Europe Coming to an End': Vienna Cardinal," 2009, http://www.lifesitenews.com/ldn/2009/apr/09041410.html

Wilson, Ralph F., "Amazing Grace: The Story of John Newton, Author of America's Favorite Hymn," Joyful Heart Renewal Ministries, http://www.joyfulheart.com/misc/newton.htm

Yancey, Philip, *What's So Amazing About Grace?* (Grand Rapids: Zondervan, 1997).

ABOUT THE AUTHOR

Rev. Dr. Stephen A. Mcallister is the founder of Spirit Renewal Ministries, a ministry devoted to transforming lives and renewing communities (www. spiritrenewalministries.com; e-mail: srministries@gmail. com). His recent research has focused on the areas of Wesleyan / holiness theology and the renewal of declining mainline liberal Protestant churches.

Stephen is a minister with the Fellowship of Christian Assemblies of Canada (http://www.fcachurches.net/). Previously he served as a minister of the United Church of Canada with congregations in New Brunswick, Newfoundland, and Ontario.

He is a graduate of the Ecumenical Doctor of Ministry program at Catholic Theological Union in Chicago, and earned a Master of Divinity degree from Queen's University, Kingston, Ontario; a Master of Business Administration degree from the Richard Ivey School of Business, University of Western Ontario, in London, Ontario; and a Bachelor of Science degree in Civil Engineering from the University of New Brunswick, Fredericton, New Brunswick.

LaVergne, TN USA
06 October 2009
160016LV00004B/3/P